Ninjutsu
The Secret Art
of the Ninja

Ninjutsu
The Secret Art of the Ninja

SIMON YEO

THE CROWOOD PRESS

First published in 2007 by
The Crowood Press Ltd
Ramsbury, Marlborough
Wiltshire SN8 2HR

www.crowood.com

This impression 2011

British Library Cataloguing-in-Publication Data
A catalogue record for this book is available from the British Library.

ISBN 978 1 86126 938 6

Disclaimer
Please note that the author and the publisher of this book are not
responsible in any manner whatsoever for any damage or injury of any
kind that may result from practising, or applying, the principles, ideas,
techniques and/or following the instructions/information described
in this publication. Since the physical activities described in this book
may be too strenuous in nature for some readers to engage in safely, it
is essential that a doctor be consulted before undertaking training.

Acknowledgements
Everything is owed to Hatsumi Soke who sowed the seeds of thought in the
first instance. I would like to thank Ali for her love and support in my thirst
for martial knowledge, and for putting up with my weeks away pursuing
this quest; also for her help with the photos. Also my agents Jen and Jane,
for their help and encouragement. I would also like to thank my brother-
in-arms, Jon Farriss, for all his encouragement, interest, and his mutually
expanding conversations that I value so much. I would also like to give
a big thank you to Paul Richardson for all his technical information and
help. Also Peter King for his friendship, for having the patience to teach me
in the first place, and for being a great travel companion. Lastly I would
like to thank Kid, my sister, for her support and help with the photos.

Typeset in Plantin by Bookcraft Ltd, Stroud, Gloucestershire

Printed and bound in India by Replika Press Pvt. Ltd.

Contents

Introduction

About the Book

In writing this book on Ninjutsu my aim is to help improve the reader's mental and physical skills and reduce weakness in both these areas. This will bring a balance to them, thus addressing the equilibrium of mind, body and spirit. Issues of harmony of the mind and body will be covered, and how one can unbalance the other. Also this book will give solutions to martial artists and to the public in general; and will explain how Ninjutsu enables you to defeat someone much bigger and stronger than yourself. As well as showing you how to perform each technique, how it works – the principles behind it – will be revealed, so that you can see for yourself how and why it is effective. How to use effective distancing to counter speed and power will be covered; how, with good timing, you can make techniques feel effortless; and how you can take a person's balance so that the outcome of a fight is no longer determined by who is stronger or faster. Principles not previously mentioned in any other martial arts books will be disclosed.

Takamatsu Sensei, the previous Ninjutsu Grand Master, said that the techniques included in this book make up the backbone of the fighting arts. If these moves are mastered and the small details understood, the reader would really be at a very high skill level.

The previous Soke, or Grand Master, has also said that, to experience ultimate happiness, you must let go of all worries and regrets, and realize that being happy is the most satisfying of life's feelings. He says you should reflect on all progress you have had in your life, and allow the positive, creative and joyous thoughts to outshine and eclipse any sorrow or grief that may be hiding in the recesses of your mind. He goes on to say that the key to overcoming adversity with a calm and happy spirit is being aware that disease and disaster occur as natural parts of life, and accepting this. Happiness is waiting there, before you, but only *you* can decide whether or not you choose to experience it.

I am also conscious that once concepts and principles are written down they become fixed. However, this is not the nature of Ninjutsu. The reader should use this book as a reference book on the way to perform the techniques in a basic way, but by no means the only way.

About Ninjutsu

The Western world has an incorrect image of the Ninja as assassins, dressed in black wearing a hood that only reveals their eyes, and running around with a sword on their back. This is largely due to all the different films and media of the 1980s that portray the Ninja in this light, and bears no relation to reality. This can also be said about the fighting styles exhibited in these aforementioned films, which are nothing more than karate mixed with acrobatics.

A Ninja is a person who has cultivated the spirit of *Ninniku*: that is, a compassionate heart, one who does not harbour grudges and who always seeks peace and harmony. In a famous historical Ninjutsu document called *The Bansenshukai* it is written that an essential trait for the Ninja is to have a pure and honest heart. It goes on to say that if a Ninja pursues a life involving lying, cheating and plotting their heart cannot be pure, and therefore their judgement will always be incorrect and their nature will never allow them to make the correct decision. A person who uses Ninjutsu for dishonest reasons or for their own personal gain may have some limited, immediate success, but will eventually be exposed for what they are. Integrity is the key point here.

It is this spiritual aspect that makes Ninjutsu so intriguing and mysterious – yet it is this very aspect that is often omitted by some instructors and many other martial arts. In my opinion without this content, the practitioner is missing out on 50 per cent of the possible cultivation. If you do not consider this part of Ninjutsu, or of humanity for that matter, it will be very easy to become just a collector of techniques, with little depth of understanding and this attitude is little better than being a hoarder of things, which can include money.

The next trait is unending perserverance. The practitioner should have an extremely high level of endurance, and it is this aspect that will help the trainee succeed when normal people would not consider the task ahead possible. There is not a prerequisite for talent, as there is no correlation between talent and effort. Effort alone can defeat the most gifted master. A lack of talent should not cause you to despair, but should provoke a commitment to work with even more effort.

The last trait is to have a curious mind. This will engender good general knowledge, common sense and a critical judgement, which in turn will give the practitioner a cultural knowledge and the ability to traverse through the hierarchy of society, as well as through different cultures without exposing themselves or offending anyone. It is not enough to be intellectual, but this intellect needs to be used, along with cultural knowledge, in practical ways. If you develop intellect with a pure intent, ultimately this will lead to spiritual refinement – which brings us back to the first trait.

I will discuss these traits in detail later on in this book.

About the Author

I have been studying martial arts since 1974, and these include Judo, Kyokushin Karate, Tai Chi and Pak Mei kung fu, Tae Kwon Do, traditional Jiu-Jitsu and currently Bujinkan Ninjutsu and Brazilian Jiu-Jitsu. At the time of writing I hold a 10th-degree black belt in Bujinkan Ninjutsu. I began training in Ninjutsu in 1987 after a long background in most other martial arts, and immediately felt Ninjutsu to be the art I had been looking for all along. It filled in all the gaps. I found it to be very efficient, and much more reliant on technique than on strength and power. Ninjutsu incorporates weapons, pressure points, punching, kicking, locking and throwing, which encompassed a lot of what I had learnt already, but in a more formalized form and without a lot of superfluous movement. It taught me how to use good distancing, to first take a person's balance, and then apply technique with good timing, rather than just struggle with my opponent and overpower them with strength.

In 1990 I started travelling round the world to train with Ninjutsu Grand Master Hatsumi Masaaki. Each year I would make four journeys, either to a long weekend of training at events called 'Tai Kai', staged around the world, or to Japan, to train with the living source of Ninjutsu. Most martial arts do not have the good fortune of having a living Grand Master, and as a consequence the art of Bujinkan Ninjutsu is still evolving, and alive, where most other arts are repetitions of historic moves, and the techniques are inappropriate in today's environment.

I was awarded my teaching licence by Hatsumi Sensei in 1994, and currently teach twice a week in London.

I would like to say at this point that I am only a conduit to the Grand Master, and my role is to prepare any student to a position where he is able to *begin* to comprehend what Hatsumi Soke and his Shihan are teaching. I would like to stress that the points I make in this book are my observations at my current level of understanding – but as we are all continually learning, these views may change or certainly evolve as time goes by.

To train with Hatsumi Soke is an amazing experience. The classes are conducted in a very light-hearted, open fashion and are not at all austere, as you would think. When you watch Soke move, it is as if he is walking round his opponents, and they are falling over. Often you are convinced that a wrist lock is doing the technique, but in reality it is a leg control, or vice versa. The opponent is always controlled on many levels physically and mentally, as well as on different vertical planes, and Soke will create a space between him and the aggressor, for that person to fall down, by discretely stealing their balance.

When Soke talks it will often be in a multi-levelled fashion, much like a parable. I remember him saying something once and thinking I understood the gist of it, but when I reflected on his words some five or so years later I realized he meant something much deeper as well. So whatever level you are on,

The author with Hatsumi Sensei at the Hombu Dojo, Japan.

his words will have some meaning, but the more you ponder them, and as you evolve as a human being as well as a martial artist, the deeper you will realize is their meaning.

History

I don't want to spend too much time on the history of Ninjutsu, as it is well documented in other books. However, I will outline a brief history so as to give the reader a basic insight into the evolution of Ninjutsu.

Ninjutsu was born out of a necessity to survive, and was developed by the rural people living in the mountains of Japan, who had a different belief system to the ruling Samurai class. Like many minorities throughout history, these people were persecuted by the ruling classes. It is not fair to say that all Ninjas were assassins and spies; however, some certainly were. By incorporating fighting techniques from exiled Chinese priests and warriors hiding in the mountains, and by adapting Samurai ju-jutsu and the people's affinity with nature, a very effective method of survival evolved; this included very efficient methods of armed and unarmed combat.

Because of the poor natural prevailing conditions, and also as a result of the widespread persecution, these people would travel all over Japan in search of work. For a few, these travelling workers were a convenient network of observers or, some might say, spies.

The Togakure Ryu school of Ninjutsu can be traced back over nine hundred years from Grand Master or Soke to Grand Master to the current Soke and my teacher, Hatsumi Masaaki. It is traditional for the Soke to pass his scrolls, or *densho*, to the next Soke along with the oral instructions, and there is an unbroken lineage stretching back thirty-four generations, as detailed here:

1. Togakure Daisuke (aka Nishina)
2. Shima Kosanta Minamoto No Kanesada
3. Togakure Goro
4. Togakure Kosanta
5. Koga Kisanta
6. Kaneko Tomoharu
7. Togakure Ryuho
8. Togakure Gakuun
9. Kido Koseki
10. Iga Tenryu
11. Ueno Rihei
12. Ueno Senri
13. Ueno Manjiro
14. Iizuka Saburo
15. Sawada Goro
16. Ozaru Ippei
17. Kimata Hachiro
18. Kataoka Heizaemon
19. Mori Ugenta
20. Toda Gogei
21. Kobe Seiun
22. Momochi Kobei
23. Tobari Tenzen
24. Toda Seiryu Nobutsuna
25. Toda Fudo Nobuchika
26. Toda Kangoro Nobuyasu
27. Toda Eisaburo Nobumasa
28. Toda Shinbei Masachika
29. Toda Shingoro Masayoshi
30. Toda Daigoro Chikashige
31. Toda Daisaburo Chikashige
32. Toda Shinryuken Masamitsu
33. Takamatsu Toshitsugu
34. Hatsumi Masaaki

The theory on the founding of the Togakure Ryu is as follows: Togakure Daisuke created the Togakure Ryu by combining his Shugendo training with the Ninja skills he learnt from Kagakure Doshi aka Kain Doshi. In the beginning there was Daisuke, Shima Kosanta Minamoto No Kanesada, a samurai who worked with Daisuke in the employment of a Shogun called Kiso Yoshinaka, and his son Rokosuke.

It is accepted that the 3rd Soke, Togakure Goro, was the person who formed the Togakure Ryu into the Ninjutsu system that is still taught today. It has been suggested that the Togakure Ryu was involved in the defence of Iga in 1581. In the 1600s the Ryu was then taught at the Hatori Ryu to the warriors of the Kishu fief. It was at this time that the Toda family, who were also Sokes of the Kumogakure Ryu, took over the Sokeship of the Togakure Ryu as well.

The 11th, 12th and 13th Sokes changed their name to that of a large town in the Iga province, Ueno. It was quite normal at this time to change your name, or be named after the town or village you came from. The Iga province is the famous province associated with the Ninja.

The 22nd Soke, Momochi Kobei, was related to Momochi Sandayu, who was the Soke of the Momochi Ryu, Gyokko Ryu and Koto Ryu (the last two ryu are also part of the Bujinkan). He was also a very important person within the Iga Ryu.

The 33rd Soke, Takamatsu Toshitsugu, belonged to the Toda family, as his grandfather was the 32nd Soke, Toda Shinryuken Masamitsu.

Hatsumi Soke is currently the Grand Master of nine different schools, or *ryu*. These schools make up the Bujinkan system and are listed below.

1. Togakure Ryu Ninjutsu
2. Gyokko Ryu Koshijutsu
3. Kukishinden Ryu Happo Hikenjutsu
4. Shinden Fudo Ryu Dakentaijutsu
5. Gyokushin Ryu Ninjutsu
6. Gikan Ryu Koppo Taijutsu
7. Koto Ryu Koppojutsu
8. Takagi Yoshin Ryu Jutaijutsu
9. Kumogakure Ryu Ninjutsu

As you can see, there are six schools of Ju-Jutsu and three schools of Ninjutsu. I am going to show you elements of the Bujinkan system, which is made from an amalgamation of all the schools, but a few in particular.

Attitude

Mental Attitude

Takamatsu Soke wrote that the essence of all martial arts and military strategies is to protect oneself, and the art of Ninjutsu fully epitomizes this concept of self-protection since it deals with the protection of the physical body as well as the mind and spirit. He also said that the way of the Ninja is the way of enduring, surviving and prevailing over all that would destroy a person; and that Ninjutsu is more than merely delivering strikes and slashes, and much deeper in significance than the simple outwitting of an opponent: it is a way of attaining what you need while making the world a better place.

When I talk about techniques and tactics, please don't just think about it from the aspect of fighting, but try to work out how the lesson applies to your work, your life and your relationships. And when I talk about 'taking balance' you should also consider how you can take your opponent's balance on a mental level. This art is so much bigger than just fighting.

Controlling the Emotions

Hatsumi Sensei has often said that '... the difference between animals and humans is that humans are able to control their instincts or emotions. If a person is unable to do this, they are no more than a wild animal.' If you are unable to control your emotions you will easily relinquish control of your feelings to someone else, giving them control of you. This is unwise in any area of life, let alone in a violent confrontation. Say, for example, that you succumb to a fit of road rage: the scenario is a person who is clearly behaving in an idiotic manner, and behaving aggressively towards you: if you choose to get angry you are allowing that person to make you feel a certain way, and you hand over the control of your feelings to someone you have previously established as being a fool. So you will have to question who is the greater fool.

Other emotions or feelings that are easily manipulated are greed and ego. It is amazing what people will engage in if they are offered easy money or are flattered sexually, in a way that shows poor judgement and is quite out of character. Again, if you can't control yourself, you won't be able to see the situation in its entirety (the bigger picture) or, again, will be easily manipulated. Neither of these is an ideal situation, whether in work, life or fighting.

Ultimately, I think the human being must learn to identify the form or structure of a situation, which is the emotionless, logical reaction to it. Before they can be creative, which relies on their instincts, they need to re-educate their instinct. It is very much like learning a new sport or art where you have to learn the basic moves or techniques before you 'free form', when you perform as an expert. Some people have naturally good instincts, but most people's instincts can be improved upon. Once you have control of your emotions you will be able to see events for what they are, without any preconceived views or wrongly anticipated outcomes, and will stop fulfilling roles that are based on illogical desires. By balancing your emotions with logic you can form a balanced view of situations and events. By remaining calm you will also be able to make the most of all the techniques and knowledge you have, which are easily blocked by emotional tension. Both these qualities are invaluable in life, and particularly in times of conflict. This has been described as 'quietening the conscious mind', or *Mu Shin*, to allow the all-knowing subconscious mind to bleed through.

The conscious mind has a tendency to 'chatter' like a monkey and obscure the subconscious mind, which recollects everything you have ever seen, heard or learnt. How many times have you got flustered and not been able to find the correct words? As always, the balance is between two extremes – in this case the emotions or instinct, as opposed to logic. If you can unbalance your opposition, your battle is already won; and if you can prevent your opposition unbalancing your mind, at least your battle is half won.

Dealing with Stress
Let us also talk about stress, and the mechanism for dealing with it. Generally there are two types of problem that cause stress: those you can influence, and those you can't. It is really important to forget the problems that you have no influence over: by definition you can't influence their outcome, so to worry about them serves no purpose. The second type of problem is the one you can influence, and it is really important to decide on your line of action as fast as possible based on the information available. And if further information becomes available, then it is quite all right to adapt your original decision. As Theodore Roosevelt commented: 'In any moment of decision, the best thing you can do is the right thing, the next best thing is the wrong thing, and the worst thing you can do is nothing.'

Hand in hand with forgetting the problems you can't influence is the issue of living in the present. Too many people worry about 'in the future this could happen, or not happen' – and again, this is a waste of energy. Clearly there needs to be some allowance for the future, but all too quickly time can pass you by. You need to enjoy the present because it is lost forever, and the future may never come. The future is a fantasy, the past is a memory, the 'now' is a gift: that is why it is called the present.

Banishing Insecurity
Lastly let us consider the human condition of relying on a person or people to make them feel a certain way. The onus on how you feel

is your own responsibility. In particular this observation relates to partners and how they interact together. For example; both partners treat each other with respect and courtesy, but one partner proclaims that the other 'doesn't love them enough', and thinks that if their partner did XYZ or behaved in a certain manner, this would prove that they did. This feeling is not based on anything to do with reality, it is based purely on how they feel and perceive their relationship. But insecurity is a feeling you *choose* to feel, and unless your partner has given you a quantifiable reason to feel insecure, you should have the ability to dispel it.

The other example comprises of people who cannot spend time on their own, or who always need to be around other people to make them feel a certain way. This is a feeling of being incomplete without a partner. A relationship cannot work properly unless two people come together as complete people, without the baggage of this inadequacy and the need for a partner to fulfil their emotional inadequacies. These people also need to rid themselves of this insecurity and become comfortable with themselves, and make themselves more balanced individuals.

Taking Control of Yourself

For sure, to address any of these issues will take work and time, but unless you can rid yourself of such feelings or needs, you cannot view circumstances from a natural balanced position. The first step in taking control of yourself is to realize that these things are happening to you, and then try to address your weaknesses. You have to decide to stop reacting in a Pavlovian fashion to the whims of your mind. When you start trying you may not at first succeed, so initially you should try with situations that are not too stressful. Look at it in the same way as you might when competing in a sport: you don't want your first competition to be the Olympics – it

is best that you start with some easier competitions first, and build up to more difficult ones after a little practice.

I found a simple way of starting to make adjustments to my emotions and to my feelings was to work on my mood. When you wake up in the morning, as long as you do not suffer from a clinical illness, you can decide to feel happy or miserable. This means that, as long as you consider this to be a logical decision, when you feel depressed, either you can choose to indulge the mood and have a really bad day, or you can take three deep breaths and decide to change your mood and have a fantastic day. After all, why would anyone choose to have a bad day? As Lance Armstrong, the seven-times winner of the Tour de France said after he survived cancer, 'Now I only have good days and great days!' I really do think that with practice you can decide how you wish to feel.

As you can see, in both Ninjutsu and in life, it is vital that you are in control of your feelings and desires, rather than your feelings and desires being in control of you. Your attitude can be your greatest weapon in life or in combat, or it can be your worst enemy. It is your choice as to which.

Physical Attitude

Controlling the Distance

The most important physical strategy is to control the distance. If you can maintain a distance beyond your opponent's punching and kicking range he will always have to make a step before being able to hit you with either his feet or his hands, and this takes away some of the reliance on superfast reactions. If you let someone get within this striking range you have to rely totally on speed and reactions to defend yourself – which is fine if you are gifted and young, but these attributes are likely to disappear with age. I think it makes good sense to train in something you can get better at with age, rather than training for years in something where you won't, and then you start being whipped by the new young beginners.

Whoever makes the first attack naturally puts themselves in a position of vulnerability, so from a martial arts perspective, it is wise to take advantage of this and control the distance to draw your opponent to make the first attack, unless you can be sure of a pre-emptive strike. The former method will also keep you, in the main, on the right side of the law. However, from a sports perspective this is not ideal, as you are scored on aggression and you also have limited time. This is the beginning of the divergence between a martial art as opposed to a combat sport. As already mentioned, speed and power disappear as you get older, so in a martial art as opposed to a sport fighting art, you have a chance of getting better as you get older because you don't have to rely so heavily on speed and power.

The other important difference between a martial art and a sport is, of course, that the sportsman wonders how to win, while the martial artist is thinking of how to survive. The consequences are also different, in that for a sports martial artist, if they lose they consider training harder in order to win the next time; but if a martial artist loses, the potential consequence is death.

The Importance of Timing
The next important skill is timing, and choosing the correct time to do your technique, be it a block or an attack. If you get your timing wrong, you will have to work that much harder to compensate. This can mean that after a few exchanges you will either be physically tired, or you will be hopelessly out of position from over-compensating; either way you are playing into the hands of your opponent. Undoubtedly you have experienced that technique, be it a throw or strike,

where you have used no effort, but your opponent has flown through the air. This is the feeling you should strive for every time in your training. There is a tendency to start with bad timing, and then to compensate with strength and power. However, if you find yourself getting tired during technique training this is a sure sign that something is wrong, and you should look carefully at your timing. The ethos of training hard and sweating a lot can be good, but it can also be misdirected, and may even be ingraining poor timing and technique. It is important therefore to analyse *how* you are training, and whether it is efficient or not. Also always seek the advice of a qualified instructor.

Linked with this is using your whole body to do a technique, by which I mean putting your body behind each technique. It is a common habit to rely on the smaller muscle groups such as your biceps and triceps to perform a move. If you can use your whole body to block, strike and throw you will find your power to be devastating, and also effortless. If your body is stationary and you punch with just your arms, you can develop some power. If you now do the same punch but at the same moment of impact you are moving your body in the same direction as the punch, for example by stepping, the force of the punch will be more than doubled.

We have looked at distancing and timing; let us now consider how we could use the principles in everyday life. This is very much like Sun Tzu's advice of crossing the river at the narrowest point, meaning that there are certain moments when it is easier to get things done than it is at other times. When things are difficult or awkward, use your knowledge of distancing and timing to choose the easiest moment to achieve what you want, or to present yourself, or to make a suggestion to someone, if you like. If you do this at the wrong time you can make all the effort, but be unsuccessful. A crude example of this is if you want to make a business appointment it would be unwise to call the client last thing on Friday, as they may well be preoccupied with going home for the weekend.

In Japanese martial arts, the unification of mind, body and technique is referred to as 'Shin Gi Tai'. If our minds are distracted by some of the issues mentioned earlier in this book, you can never have this unified state of being. Singing is an example, because if you don't put spirit into the performance, the song will be lifeless even though technically it was performed perfectly. Hatsumi Sensei suggests that rather than seeking this unification of mind, body and technique on a daily basis, you should try and attain it when you are attempting to do something specific that requires it. This is the value of *Mu Shin* or 'no mind', trying to empty your mind of any self-constraining thoughts or emotions.

The Complete Human Being

With regard to these physical and mental attitudes, one might say that you can master a thousand opponents, but first you must master yourself. It has also been said that the human being should forge themselves like a sword, with continuous tempering, sharpening and polishing. I believe this refers to the mind, body and spirit, and one or two aspects of the three are often omitted. People are happy to focus on one or two of these and omit working on the remainder – and some don't work on any of them at all. For some reason people often attend to these issues when they have lost someone close to them or have suffered an illness or injury. But it should not take such dramatic circumstances to provoke introspection; and also by its nature, another aspect has been removed or damaged, so that aspect is now difficult to work on. This circumstance again leaves the person incomplete, although now in a different way. I think it is very important to work continuously on all

three aspects, so you can evolve as a complete human being.

Ninjutsu: a Comparison

The fact that I have studied a number of different arts, as mentioned above (including Judo, Karate, Kung Fu, Tae Kwon Do, traditional Jiu-Jitsu and Brazilian Jiu-Jitsu), gives me the opportunity to be objective about tai jutsu or the unarmed fighing techniques of Ninjutsu. Bujinkan Ninjutsu is a comprehensive art in that it teaches the elements of punching and kicking, and locking and throwing, as well as various weapons. As the Grand Master is still alive, the art is still evolving, and at higher levels, defence against current weapons is taught. The footwork taught in Ninjutsu is second to none, and is often a rather random affair in other arts. Once you have studied Ninjutsu to black belt you can begin to see how other martial arts' techniques can be applied in a Ninjutsu style. Ninjutsu is also a martial art, as opposed to a sport, and more will be written about this later on.

There are specific weapons used in Ninjutsu, and what is remarkable is how, once you have an understanding of the unarmed fighting, using these weapons becomes a natural extension of your body and all you have previously learnt. Like physics there are certain rules and principles and, as long as you apply these, you can use them in variations, or *henka*, of a specific technique. As mentioned earlier, the art of taking your opponent's balance prior to applying technique is another cornerstone of this art, and combining this with using your whole body to apply techniques makes Ninjutsu a devastating but, equally, a logical and scientific art.

Once you have been training in this art for some years and have learnt the correct and logical ways of doing things, there will come a time when you will need to pass the fifth

Dan and the teaching licence test, which will rely totally on your esoteric skills. The test requires you to kneel on the ground in front of the Grand Master with your back to him; he is holding a *shinai* or bamboo sword in a raised position. At an unspecified time the Grand Master will try and hit you on the top of your head. It is up to you to feel his intention and roll out of the way without being hit, thus passing the test. If you roll prematurely or get hit you fail. The only advice I can give a prospective candidate is to go mentally to zero, and to clear their mind of extraneous thoughts. If you think of passing or failing you will surely fail. This is *Mu Shin*. When I did my test I used exactly this technique and rolled out of the way on the first attempt – although at that precise moment it felt as if time stood still and I was pushed out of the way. At no point do I remember consciously deciding to roll out of the way. The following two weeks left me very confused as to what had occurred. After a period of reflection I began to realize that I had to forget my scientific education and accept that this was something that I could not explain scientifically. Please don't think that there is anything too remarkable with this test. I believe everyone can do this, it is just that most of us have forgotten how to react to this kind of stimulus.

In short, I have found the Bujinkan system very efficient at cultivating physical and esoteric attributes, and Hatsumi Sensei's teachings have helped me very much, personally, both in my life and in business, as well as being a totally fascinating art.

I hope that once you understand the principles and rules I am going to divulge, it will start you on your way to being a great martial artist. The word 'artist' implies that you create something unique, and don't just regurgitate old historic techniques: please remember this as you progress.

Training with Hatsumi Sensei

There are quite a few things that have stayed in my mind after training with the Grand Master; one of them is the encouragement to keep going. To persevere sounds like a very basic instruction, but it is one where most people fall by the wayside, and so fail to fulfil their dreams and desires. If you want to be good at anything, whether it is martial arts, a job or life, you have to persevere and keep pushing forwards. Sometimes you will feel as if you are standing still or treading water, but if you don't try to move forwards, you will go backwards. And as far as training is concerned, it is vital that you keep turning up to class, even when you are injured or tired: it will give you a chance to rest the injured area and train the other areas, which in normal situations may not be so strong. 'Persevering heart' is also one of the meanings of the Japanese word *nin* that is part of the word 'Ninjutsu'. I am sure that ever since Hatsumi Sensei started teaching, people have asked him about the so-called secrets of Ninjutsu, and he has always replied *gambatte*, or to 'keep going', and the more I train the more I realize how true this is. It is so important to persevere and to keep training, even when you least feel like it.

On this subject Hatsumi Sensei has written that you should forget your sadness, anger, grudges and hatred: they should be allowed to pass like smoke caught in a breeze. Also that you should not deviate from the path of righteousness, and should lead a life worthy of a man, and not be possessed by greed, luxury or your ego. He goes on to say that you should accept sorrows, sadness and hatred as they are, and should consider them as a trial, given to you by the powers, a blessing from nature. You should have your mind and your time fully engaged in *budo*, and your mind deeply set on *bujutsu*.

15

Hatsumi Sensei has also said that, if everything seems to be going wrong, you should go back to basics, since these are the fundamentals of what you understand. In martial arts terms I would like this to be the content of this book; on a business level this may be your core business: it is really what has always worked for you in the past. I think it is very easy for a person to over-complicate things, be it in training or in life, and as a consequence things can get so complicated and muddled, that they can eventually stop working. At this point, therefore, it is time to revert to basics and to start building up again. It is the same with training; where progress is being made at a reasonable rate, suddenly all the techniques may seem to stop working so well, and it is at this point that you should revisit the basic techniques that make up your style. You may have started over-complicating things.

Balance is also talked about a lot, and has already been mentioned earlier in this introduction. On a basic level this obviously means your physical balance, and maintaining your balance while endeavouring to steal your opponent's stability. At any time during training that you feel out of balance, then something is undoubtedly wrong. This can be a very useful training tool for self analysis. Balance is also about the way you should lead your life, not doing anything to extreme or excess, and having balance in all that you do. Often a lot of truths can be discovered as you observe the balance between all the information available.

Nowadays Hatsumi Sensei is no longer really teaching *Waza* or technique: he is teaching what happens in a fight after technique, trying to find the best in an imperfect situation. This is what happens after technique, maybe when things don't work out perfectly, how to make sure the result turns out in your favour. This style of teaching is very difficult to understand, as there isn't really anything to understand: it is an acceptance of how to take advantage of situations or your opponent's mistakes, and capitalize on them, all within the framework of the technique. Within this you have to really understand the Waza intimately. It is the Waza within the Waza, and how to move and react in a natural way. It has been said that this type of training is beyond solely Waza or technique, and is about controlling the *kukan*, or space between and around the combatants.

1 Principles

Kazushi (Breaking Balance)

If you are involved in a fight it is vital to take your opponent's balance first, before applying any type of technique (meaning strikes as well as locks and throws). If you do not abide by this rule the conflict will always be two people opposing each other, and the strongest, fastest person will win: there will be little chance for the smaller, weaker person to be able to defeat the larger, stronger opponent. This concept is absolutely the cornerstone of Ninjutsu training, because without it, the fight becomes a non-technical display of brute force and it is vital that this is avoided.

To take someone's balance you need to apply pressure in the direction of a line perpendicular to a line drawn between the opponent's heels. If you push anyone in this direction they will always need to take a step to regain their balance.

If an assailant attacks you, you should move him in the direction described above to take his balance, and at this point, when he is off balance and unable to attack you effectively, you should apply your strike, lock or throw. Logically, the best time to apply your technique is when your opponent can't attack you effectively because they are off balance.

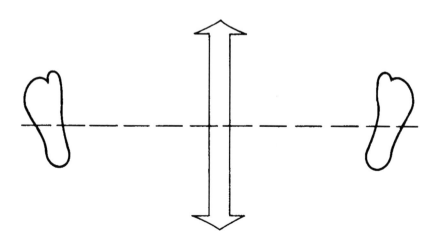

The direction to break a person's balance is perpendicular to a line drawn between the person's feet: if you push or pull them in this direction they will stumble.

This makes perfect sense, yet in a lot of arts it is completely forgotten.

This is the principle; how to take your opponent's balance physically is described in the technical part of this book. You should attempt to break an opponent's *kamae*, or posture, progressively, through a series of techniques, rather than look for one single knock-out technique. Once you have manoeuvred the opponent to a position where he is severely off balance, then you can take him with a strike, lock or throw. Conversely, I have seen practitioners who are excellent at systematically breaking their opponent's *kamae* but who never actually take the finishing technique. Do not be afraid to apply a finishing move, be it a finishing strike, lock or throw. But equally, don't be too eager.

If you can master this balance breaking, it is quite feasible to throw your opponent by using subtle movements without touching him. This is the principle of the *Kuki Nage*, or air/void throw, which relies on you moving in such a way that you take the opponent's balance while allowing him to believe that if he reaches a bit further he will be able to either hit or grab you. It is essentially making the opponent feel he can achieve what he wants, and making him over-commit to that end, at the expense of his balance.

Don't forget about taking your assailant mentally off balance as well as physically off balance. This can be done by simply asking the aggressor questions; and remember to give your opponent a way out so he can retain some face. If you don't give him this way out, you will end up psychologically cornering him and, in the same way as a rat that has been cornered by a cat, he will end up attacking you. Giving people a face-saving way out is a very important psychological skill to apply in any conflict, so as to avoid physical combat.

Use Your Whole Body

The concept here is to use your whole body to strike, block or throw – *ken tai ichi*, the weapon and body as one. As already mentioned, logically, why use some of the weakest muscles of the body, the muscles of the arms, when you could use these muscles along with those of the whole body? In the same way more power can be added to kicks – though to a lesser degree due to the natural strength of the legs – by putting the whole body behind each kick. Co-ordinating your movement does this, so you can utilize the power from your whole body when punching, kicking, applying locks and throwing. The idea is to be able to knock your opponent off their feet when you hit them.

Hatsumi Sensei often says 'punch using your knees' or 'punch with your whole body', and obviously this used to cause considerable confusion. However, what he means is to incorporate the movement and muscles of the ankles, knees, core muscles and the whole body *behind the punching action*. This concept should be applied to defensive blocks, and all movements where you need to generate power: power should be a natural product of body movement, not muscular tension. Again, how to use the whole body physically will be demonstrated later in the book.

You should strive for natural body movement, and this should be so thoroughly a part of the techniques that you no longer have to think about them – they should flow from you freely, without thought. This is very different to trying to pre-conceive an attack and work out your responses. Of course you can only expect this flow of technique to be the correct solution to an attack if your perception is correct, and you are not mentally off balance, as discussed before.

Nagare (Flow of Technique)

Another point often neglected is the flow from one technique to the next. Generally when a technique fails to work because the opponent resists, it is time to flow into another technique, more often than not in the direction the opponent is resisting. Often what happens is the practitioner will try a technique and the opponent resists, and the defender continues to insist on the original technique: he then either gets hit or, one way or another, the technique fails.

This is when a lot of people think that certain techniques don't work; however, it is at this point that the practitioner should have considered flowing into another technique. It is also this flow in technique that is needed at more advanced levels to overcome a skilled opponent. You can lead your adversary in one direction and force him to defend one attack, knowing his defence will expose him or leave him vulnerable to another attack from a different direction. You can also expect him to counter your second attack, but leave himself open to yet a different attack: the counter to the counter, if you like. It is this continuous flow that will enable you to catch your opponent out at some point. This continuous flow is also what is needed to progressively break down the opponent's *kamae* or posture. Figuratively speaking this is like the river flowing down a mountain, in that when it comes upon obstacles it is not held up by them, but moves around them and continues on. This is the principle of nagare.

Angling

This is vitally important for both defence and attack. Without proper angling you will not be able to satisfactorily or effectively avoid an attack or deliver an efficient counter technique. As far as defensive manoeuvres are concerned within the Bujinkan, you should move away either linearly or in a circular fashion at a 45-degree angle or sideways – basically moving off the line of attack. If this is done correctly it will generally leave you in the correct position to counter attack with the correct angle and distancing. This angle is in a direction where you can apply your technique efficiently and at the same time take your opponent's balance, and this principle applies for strikes as well as locks and throws. (This is generally in the direction shown in the illustration on page 17.)

As with all principles in the Bujinkan style of Ninjutsu, there are general principles, but they are not inflexible. As Hatsumi Soke has said: 'If martial arts have a rigid structure, at some time something will come along that will shatter that structure.' You need to be flexible in your thoughts and responses. This will also help you come up with surprise techniques, and avoid becoming staid and predictable. Remember, evasiveness comes from just subtle adjustments of body position. You should also consider moving just enough to convince the opponent that he will hit you. This will cause him to overreach in his eagerness to strike you and cause him to lose his balance.

Non-Compliant Opponents

As already mentioned, too many people are seen to apply a technique against an opponent and, when he resists, they continue to persist with the technique, the opponent continues to resist, and the person doing the technique writes it off as one that does not work. There are two things happening here. Firstly, as previously discussed, the opponent's balance has not been taken effectively, and he still has a base or platform to resist from. Given this – and sometimes mistakes are made and you don't take the opponent's balance fully – you need to distract his mind from defending the technique you are trying to apply. For example, if you are trying to apply Omote Gyaku (outside wrist twist) and he resists by locking his shoulder and elbow, you need to take his mind or focus off this defence and move it elsewhere. This can be simply done by striking into the space between his bicep and triceps on his inner arm (*jakkin*). The pain he feels – and this can be from a strike to any point – will move his focus to that point, and not on defending the wrist twist; you will then find the wrist twist will work more than adequately.

This kind of technique is not an excuse for not taking an opponent's balance properly in the first instance.

Secondly, your other solution for a non-compliant opponent, as discussed previously, is to flow into another technique in the direction that the opponent is resisting. Another solution is to use non-linear movement, as most people who understand these locks know how to resist in a general way. However, if you alter the manner in which you apply the lock, you can fool the opponent. For example, again if your opponent is resisting Omote Gyaku you should consider changing the direction of the lock into a spiral movement downwards, or use a jerking movement to finish the lock.

Kime (Intention)

Kime can also be described as 'focus' or 'intensity'. I have seen a lot of students performing beautiful techniques but without this intensity or focus, and this reduces the techniques to a dance, which is not how they should be performed. When doing any technique, alone or with a partner, focus on what you are doing and on your partner. Really try and focus your mind, and think that you are using the technique in a real situation, or certainly try and achieve that kind of intensity. This does not mean using anger or hitting your opponent hard: it means harbouring a kind of latent aggression and gives a non-physical bite to your technique. It is like a silent *ki-ai*, made from within. It is a very difficult thing to explain, but if you master it you can take an opponent's balance without touching them.

Moguri Gata (Upper and Lower Form)

This is the concept of capturing the opponent on several levels: Gedan (lower level), Chudan (middle level) and Jodan (upper level). So, for example, while you are taking a wrist lock on your opponent, it is good, for you, to try and also control his foot or leg: if you can do this and trap him in this fashion within your techniques, you will be able to really capture him. This is also relevant for striking and being able to hit low, then high, to confuse the opponent.

2 Fitness and Stretching

I am not going to write at length about *junan taiso*, or conditioning and stretching. However, it is extremely important to be physically fit and to have a good aerobic capacity. You need to have some strength with good endurance: you cannot expect to prevail in a combat situation if you do not have these qualities. For a benchmark of basic fitness you should be able to run a mile on the flat in under seven minutes. Also, being overweight stresses your load-bearing joints and causes undue wear and tear of these joints. Why spend years learning how to protect yourself from others, when you are actually doing the damage to yourself? Carrying excess weight also inhibits a lot of the movements required in Ninjutsu; the practitioner should eat natural healthy foods and will then be able to make the most of the training.

With regard to stretching, there is no need to go into too much detail here, as there are many books written by experts on this subject. However, a good technique to adopt when stretching is to go to maximum extension and then hold the stretch for a minimum of 30sec. This is because when you first stretch a muscle, it reacts by contracting and constricting. After about 10–15sec this constriction subsides and you can then start to stretch the muscle. This is why stretching for any shorter time than 30sec is useless and has no impact on the length of the muscle. This also explains why ballistic stretching, or stretching by bouncing, is more likely to hurt you than to increase the muscle length, since you are effectively trying to stretch the muscle while it is constricted.

Another stretching technique I have found useful is, when a muscle is at full stretch, contract it as hard as you can for 5sec, and then relax. This should allow you to stretch a little further. If you repeat this cycle five times you should be able to get quite a good increase in your range of stretch.

As a basic benchmark for flexibility you should be able to do the side splits in both directions as well as the box splits (facing forward). I am fully aware of how difficult the latter is to do; however, all students should always be trying to improve their flexibility at every opportunity, because without this kind of flexibility you will not be able to kick or move freely. You should endeavour to stretch every day and more if you want a good improvement. The shoulders and spine should also be flexible, and you should be able to hold your hands behind your back, one arm over your shoulder, and the other from behind your hip. Having a flexible spine and shoulders will greatly assist your escape from locks and throws, as well as your movement in general. You should also loosen up your wrists, knees, fingers, toes and ankles during the stretching process as these are areas that can be easily damaged if twisted or over-extended.

It is vital to be warmed up and your whole body fully stretched before embarking upon the techniques that follow.

3 Kamae (Postures)

Kamae is the word for 'posture' or 'stance'. There are ten different postures in the Bujinkan system, as detailed below.

For the more advanced student, the postures in Ninjutsu are more than merely positions that we choose to put our body in, to aid us during a violent confrontation: they are the physical manifestation of the individual's mental perspective. They will naturally be changing all the time during an encounter as it progresses, so they are the most appropriate at any given moment. There will be moments during a fight when we will feel aggressive, elusive or defensive. If we don't have a balanced mental perspective due to some of the issues previously discussed, then there is little chance of getting the correct mental perspective, and no chance of selecting the correct *kamae*. The importance of having a good balance between mind, body and technique should now start to become clearer; if you observe wild animals hunting, for example, their minds and bodies are unified for the specific job in hand. It seems to be only humans that suffer from a separation of this imaginary division, and who require retraining in natural movement.

The *kamae* are only recommendations of how to use the body, and should be adapted to the individual's physiology. It is important that students should not be carbon copies of their instructors, as their bodies may differ considerably. However, this doesn't mean that an idle attitude can be adopted when working on postures: they have been developed over the last thousand years, and obviously have as much value now, as they did when they were created. These stances should be worked on in a low position so the legs build strength, then if you adopt a higher stance, your legs are more powerful and agile. If you train in a high stance and have to drop your centre of gravity or lower your posture, due to a slippery floor for example, your legs will tire quickly and you will lose your agility.

As the student progresses, the importance of these postures will be internalized, and the need for the specific stances will diminish until you work without a fighting posture at all.

Seiza (Kneeling Posture)

This is a kneeling position with the knees spread a little and the toes pointing backwards; the feet are touching, so you are sitting on the soles of your feet. The hands should be placed on top of the thighs, fingers pointing inwards, and the spine and neck should be aligned vertically. This posture is a non-aggressive position and is often used in meditation.

Fudoza (Immovable Seat Posture)

In this posture the left leg is as it is in Seiza, but the right foot is placed halfway along the left calf. Again, the hands should be on the

Seiza No Kamae.

Fudoza No Kamae.

thighs, and the spine straight as for Seiza. If you were wearing Hakama it would give the illusion that you were in Seiza: however, you would be ready to deal with an attack in an instance, as the right leg is free to move.

Shizen No Kamae (Natural Posture)

The correct way to form this stance is to stand naturally, with your feet a shoulder-width apart and the knees slightly bent. The arms should hang relaxed, and the hands should be open at your sides. The spine and head should be aligned vertically.

Ichimonji No Kamae (Number One Posture)

Described here is a left (Hidari) Ichimonji from two schools, the Togakure Ryu and the Gyokko Ryu. Clearly the student needs to be able to do both sides, but here we will only look at the left side. For the Togakure Ryu version the feet need to be approximately two shoulder-widths apart. The left foot and

Shizen No Kamae.

23

Ichimonji No Kamae
(Togakure Ryu style).

Ichimonji No Kamae
(Gyokko Ryu style).

Kiten Ken or Shuto. The striking area is the edge of the hand. Also *see* page 89.

Shito Ken or Boshi Ken. The striking area is the tip of the thumb. Also *see* page 91.

knee should point forwards, and the right foot and knee should point 45 degrees backwards. There should be 75 per cent weight on the back leg, and 25 per cent weight on the front. Your body should be left side forwards, presenting as small a target as possible. Your left arm should point forwards, with fingers pointing at the opponent's eyes, and the right hand should be in *shuto*, also called Kiten Ken (*see* the photo above), at your neck, with your right elbow down, protecting your ribs.

There are other variations of this posture, such as the one found in Gyokko Ryu. This variation deviates from the previous version in that the left arm is angled slightly to the right so the back of the right hand faces the opponent. The right hand is in Shito Ken, often called Boshi Ken (*see* the photo above), and placed by the left elbow. The hand forms are covered in more detail in Chapter 8. You should stare into your opponent's eyes and have the intention of making him do whatever you want.

For the basic moves within the Bujinkan we will start by working with the Gyokko Ryu style, as this is, some say, the foundation of many schools. With all stances based on this leg position, it is important not to straighten

the knee joint of the front leg too much as it will be easily broken by a kick from your opponent.

Doko No Kamae (Angry Tiger Posture)

For this position the body is in the same position as Ichimonji No Kamae, but with the right hand held high as if holding a telephone away from the right ear. You can also hold this hand higher above the head if desired. It is important to keep the elbow of the right arm down, so as to be able to protect the ribs from any potential attack.

Hicho No Kamae (Flying Bird or Crane Posture)

For this posture, stand on your right leg with the right foot turned 90 degrees to the right. The left foot should point downwards and rest on the inside top of the right calf. The left arm points forwards, with the hand open as before, and the right hand is in Shito Ken (*see* the photo on page 26), hidden on the inside of the left elbow, with the thumb pointing upwards. A lot of people struggle with their

25

Doko No Kamae.

Hicho No Kamae.

Hira Ichimonji No Kamae.

Shikan Ken. The striking area is the edge of the second knuckles.

balance in this posture, but the solution is to keep the supporting leg slightly bent. On a more general note, if you are struggling with balance, it always pays to lower your centre of gravity by flexing your legs more. You should look into your opponent's eyes and have the intention of storing up all your energy.

Hira Ichimonji No Kamae (Flat Number One Posture)

The arms are outstretched to the sides as you face forwards. The legs should be two shoulder-widths apart, the knees should be slightly bent, and there should be even weight on both feet. You can close your fingers into Shikan Ken (*see* the photo above) to avoid having them cut off by your opponent's sword. Look into the opponent's eyes.

Hoko No Kamae (Angry Bear Posture)

In this posture the feet are one and a half shoulder-widths apart, and the left foot is slightly in front of the right, with 70 per cent of the weight on the front foot. The arms are raised above the head as if you are holding a large ball. The hands can form claws if

Hoko No Kamae.

desired. In this posture your objective is to make yourself look bigger than you are, in the same way that many animals make themselves look bigger when cornered. Again you should look into your opponent's eyes and try to find the resolve to drive all the opponent's attacks back, or to totally envelope the opponent.

Kosei No Kamae (Aggressive Energy Posture)

The lower body is in the same position as Hoko No Kamae. However, the left hand is held in Shuto (*see* the photo on page 25) over your brow, and the right hand is in Shikan Ken (*see* the photo above) over your chest. Look into your opponent's eyes.

Kosei No Kamae.

Jumonji No Kamae.

Jumonji No Kamae (Cross or Figure Ten Posture)

The lower body is in the same position as the last two postures. The arms are crossed at the wrists and held away from the chest, with the hands in Boshi Ken (*see* the photo on page 25) and the thumbs pointing upwards. Whichever leg is in front, so should be the corresponding arm. Look into your opponent's eyes, and have the intention of repelling all of his attacks.

4 Ukemi (Break Falls)

Ukemi is the method of hitting the ground safely without being injured, and is extremely useful if you are thrown, pushed, tripped or knocked to the ground by an opponent or an obstacle. You may also use these techniques to avoid an attack. It enables you to hit the ground without injuring yourself, and in most instances allows you to get straight back on your feet again, and face your opponent or run off to escape. It works by spreading the point of impact over as big a surface area as possible; in most instances this is the back.

The other benefit of rolling is the therapeutic effect it has on the back. When you first start rolling it will feel like a cube rolling over the ground. However, as you practise more, you will find that the corners disappear and this has a softening effect on your back and increases its suppleness and flexibility.

These rolling skills allow you to offer no resistance, which is a fundamental principle, and also enable you to use the circumstances to perform a counter or a movement to your advantage.

Rolling in Ninjutsu differs from rolling in other arts in that you remain looking at your opponent through the roll; this enables you to prepare for the opponent's next attack during the roll, or at least to be aware of his position and intention. The other point to bear in mind in Ninjutsu is that the rolls should be done silently; remember this is an art of stealth. The other difference is that you can also attack during the course of a roll, with weapons such as a Shuriken or your hands and feet. Please bear these points in mind through the technical part of this chapter.

Forward Roll

This is similar to head-over-heels. The idea is to roll the length of the spine, but without hitting your head. In the first instance you must support yourself with your arms and let your head turn under you, allowing the back of your shoulders to be the first point of contact with the ground. You should try and keep tight, like a ball, so you are able to keep rolling back on to your feet. Please be conscious of making gentle contact with your shoulders: you don't want to damage yourself while rolling. This is a warming-up roll to prepare for the following rolls.

Zenpo Kaiten (Forward Roll)

This is a roll over one shoulder, to the opposite hip and back on to your feet. To begin, step forward with your left leg and keep your hips low. Gradually move your weight over your left leg as you put your left palm on the ground between your legs. Now look behind you, over your right shoulder as you roll over, making the next point of contact with the ground the back of your left shoulder. You should roll across your back and on to your right hip, and up on to your feet.

Common Mistakes

The mistake most commonly made is to impact the point of the shoulder into the ground, and not the back of the shoulder. You will be aware if this is happening, as the obvious tell-tale sign is that it will hurt.

The other common mistake is that when you roll, you don't keep your feet tucked in and often have problems coming on to your feet. Again, pain is the giveaway sign, this time in your lower back or the back of your pelvis.

Forward roll

I get as low as possible, with both hands on the ground.

I am halfway through the roll, making sure I don't make any contact with my head on the ground.

I am starting to come up, bringing my hands forwards in case I need to protect myself.

Right: I make sure that at the end I come back on to my feet.

You should be able to do this with both hands touching the ground, one hand touching the ground, no hands, and diving forwards.

Ushiro Nagare (Backward Roll)

For some reason the backward roll causes a lot of people problems. This is the basic version, as demonstrated in Hatsumi Sensei's earliest video. It also enables you to get off the line between you and your opponent, and to move backwards at 45 degrees. To do this roll, stand in a natural posture with your feet a shoulder-width apart (Shizen No Kamae). Step back with your right leg directly behind your left, about two shoulder-widths apart, into Ichimonji No Kamae. Then transfer your weight on to your right leg and lower yourself gently so you are sitting by your right foot. Now lean to your right and put your head on your right shoulder, and roll backwards kicking your left leg back at 45 degrees and to the right. Come back up on to your feet.

The common variation of this technique is to lean your head to the opposite side at the start of the roll. However, this has a tendency to make you roll straight back, and does not get you off the line of attack.

Common Mistakes

A common mistake for this roll is to sit on the floor too hard, forgetting it could be concrete. It is important to lower yourself gently, using your left supporting leg. Look at a baby learning to walk, who stands and then sits down on the floor: this is the natural movement we are trying to emulate. We learn bad movements as we get older, and in a lot of Ninjutsu we are trying to recreate a natural way of moving.

Another mistake is to throw your upper body backwards instead of sideways. You can tell if this is happening because you end up rolling over your head and potentially hurting your neck. With any of the rolls your head should never touch the ground.

Yet another mistake is to throw your left leg straight back, instead of back and to the right, causing you to drop out of the roll halfway through.

Yoko Nagare (Sideways Roll)

This roll is to help you escape sideways, and is one of the easier rolls to do. To do it, start by placing the feet two shoulder-widths apart, and arms outstretched to the side (Hira Ichimonji No Kamae). Move your right leg across in front of your left, and use your left supporting leg to gently lower your buttocks to the ground. Then lean your upper body forwards and roll over your right shoulder, across your shoulders on to your left shoulder, and back on to your feet. This rolling motion should also be done while looking at the opponent all the time, or at least in front of you. It means that during a roll you are always aware of what your opponent is doing and how he is reacting. You should finish back in Hira Ichimonji No Kamae.

There are not a lot of mistakes to be made here if the instructions are followed closely, and most people find this roll quite easy to perform. Always remember to follow a sideways direction.

Zenpo Ukemi (Forward Breakfall)

Start by standing in Shizen No Kamae, and fall forwards while landing on your forearms, making sure you land all at once on to the part of the body stretching from your elbow to your palm. At the same time break at the waist a little and kick one of your legs back, to act as a counter balance. The small details here are to move your hands towards each other, but not touching, and your elbows

Zenpo Kaiten

I get as low as possible, while checking the ground in front of me.

As I roll, I look backwards and roll over my left arm to my left shoulder.

Still looking backwards, I roll from my left shoulder to my right hip.

I come up to my feet by bringing my feet close to me, and face back in Ichimonji No Kamae.

Ushiro Nagare (backward roll)

I start in Shizen No Kamae.

I gently lower myself to the ground using my supporting right leg.

I step back into Ichimonji No Kamae.

While still looking forwards, I lean to the right and start to roll backwards. Note how my head does not touch the ground.

Ushiro Nagare (backward roll) *cont*.

I am still looking backwards as my legs come over.

I come back on to my feet and assume Ichimonji No Kamae.

Yoko Nagare (sideways roll)

I am in Hira Ichimonji No Kamae.

I have started to lower myself gently using my left leg, looking forwards.

Yoko Nagare (sideways roll) *cont.*

I am rolling from my right shoulder to my left shoulder. Note how I am still looking forwards.

Even as I am finishing the roll I am still looking forwards.

As I start to come back on to my feet I am still looking forwards.

I come back into posture, Hira Ichimonji No Kamae.

away from each other a little. You should also turn your face to one side so if a mistake is made you do not impact your nose and mouth into the ground.

In the main most people find this technique quite straightforward once they have overcome the fear of falling forwards.

The next set of rolls combines postures with various rolls, and how to use these rolls in a more combative way.

Hira No Kamae

For this technique you start standing in Shizen No Kamae facing your opponent who is holding a sword above his head in Daijo-dan No Kamae. As he cuts down to your head, you step back at 45 degrees with your right leg into Ichimonji No Kamae. Leading off with your right arm, do a sideways roll. As you roll, you should keep looking back

Zenpo Ukemi (forward breakfall)

As I start to fall I prepare my forearms and start kicking up and back with my right leg.

I start in Shizen No Kamae.

Right: I have landed on my forearms, turned my face to one side, and kicked my right leg up high to counterbalance my fall.

Hira No Kamae

Uke finds the correct cutting distance, so he can cut with the first 5in (13cm) of his *boken*.

Both Uke and Tori then assume their starting postures.

at your opponent. When you come back on to your feet you should face the opponent in the Ichimonji No Kamae posture. This technique should be executed smoothly from start to finish, and not in a staccato-type style that breaks up each movement.

The above technique applies one of Ninjutsu's basic principles: when you are attacked, don't be there. You then have a choice of moving away or counter attacking.

Ichimonji No Kamae

Again you are facing your opponent, but this time you are in Ichimonji No Kamae; he is in Daijodan No Kamae, as before, with the sword raised above his head. As the opponent steps forward with his right leg and cuts to your head, do a forward roll over your right shoulder, again looking at him as you roll, and come up on to one knee.

Hira No Kamae *cont.*

As Uke cuts down, Tori moves back and to the right at 45 degrees into Ichimonji No Kamae.

Tori then does a Yoko Nagare (sideways roll). Please note how Tori is looking at Uke as he starts to roll.

Hira No Kamae *cont.*

Even through the roll Tori maintains visual contact with Uke.

Tori comes up into Ichimonji No Kamae. On this occasion it is a low version of the posture Tori has decided to adopt.

The opponent then cuts again to your head, and as he does so, you move in under the sword's hilt and strike to his abdomen with a Boshi Ken (*see* the photo on page 25). In the basic version of this technique you do not protect your head when you make the Boshi Ken strike. However, I suspect that this technique came from an era when a helmet would have been worn. I now favour protecting with my hand, to avoid being struck with the hilt or guard of the sword, as I make the Boshi Ken strike.

The above is a great example of having a living Grand Master. He is there to explain the changes over the years and how a technique should be applied, depending upon whether the people of the time were wearing armour or just a kimono.

Ichimonji No Kamae

Both Tori and Uke start in their respective postures.

As Uke cuts down, Tori does a Zenpo Kaiten (forward roll). Again Tori watches Uke during the roll.

Ichimonji No Kamae *cont.*

Even in the middle of the roll Tori watches Uke.

Tori comes up into a low Ichimonji No Kamae as Uke prepares to cut down again.

Before Uke can cut down, Tori dives in with a Boshi Ken to the stomach.

5 San Shin No Kata (The Three Heart Form)

Some say the San Shin No Kata is based on the elements earth, water, fire, wind and void. These collectively are called the Godai or the 'Big Five', and in Japanese belief they are intrinsic with nature and the formation of the Earth. Others say that the elemental names merely constitute a way of numbering the sequence. Current belief and research suggest that the latter is most likely, and that the names are just that, only names, and that no feeling of earth, water, fire, air and void should be associated with the movement.

The San Shin No Kata was a series of techniques taught exclusively by Takamatsu Sensei to the current Grand Master, Hatsumi Masaaki, and it has been said that it comes from the secret teachings of the Gyokko Ryu. When Toda Shinryuken taught this to Takamatsu Sensei, he told him that the major principle did not lie in the form, but in the heart and spirit of the practitioner. He also taught that the movement in San Shin No Kata was connected to the teaching of weapon techniques when using Katana, Shuriken, Tanto, Kusari Fundo and a gun. The body movements should be the same regardless of the weapon, or if you don't have a weapon at all. It needs to be practised in an extreme position – that is, in a lower position, with more dynamic use of the knees and exaggerating using the whole body together as a weapon, *ken tai ichi*.

Much has been said about the *San* of San Shin, which translates as 'three'. It has been said that the practitioner should maintain the heart and mind of a three year old – that is, to have the innocence, large heartedness and enthusiasm of a three-year-old child. If you approach your life, training, relationships and everything you do in this way, happiness will surely follow. Another play on the 'three' connotation is the three ways of training the San Shin No Kata:

- The first is the Soshin Go Kata, where you practise the techniques below on your own in a static horse-riding stance.
- The second is Go Gyo Kata, where you start in Shizen No Kamae and then move into Soshin No Kamae, which is like Ichimonji No Kamae but your right hand is held at your right hip in Boshi Ken, and you proceed with the techniques below. Again, this is solo practice.
- Thirdly there is the Goshin No Kata, which are the techniques detailed below, which you practise with your partner.

Don't forget to practise both left and right sides of the techniques detailed below.

Chi No Kata (Earth Form)

The defender (Tori) stands in Shizen No Kamae, and the attacker (Uke) faces him in Hidari Ichimonji No Kamae (left arm forward). Uke punches with his right fist at Uke's face. Tori steps back and to the right at 45 degrees with his right leg, and slides his left foot towards his right foot a little to avoid Uke's right foot, at the same time lifting his left arm, so his left hand makes contact with the inside of Uke's right wrist. This movement just checks Uke's punch. Tori should then move his left foot towards his right foot, and then steps forwards with his right foot while using his shoulders to swing his right arm forwards in a pendulum-like motion, to strike with a San Shin Tan Ken to Uke's solar plexus. San Shin Tan Ken is formed by touching the little finger and thumb together. The fore- and ring fingertips touch each other, and the middle fingertip reinforces them by resting on top of them (*see* page 45). The distancing for the strike should be to hit the target with an almost straight right arm.

Common Mistakes
The main mistake made with this technique is not to use the right arm as a pendulum in a natural fashion. Tori should really work on a low posture and the dynamic use of the knees to get a deceptively large amplitude of movement. He should really work on throwing the San Shin Tan Ken strike with his shoulders.

Sui No Kata (Water Form)

Tori and Uke face each other. Uke stands in Hidari Ichimonji No Kamae, and Tori is in Hidari Soshin No Kamae. Soshin No Kamae is the same as Ichimonji No Kamae, except the right hand is held at the hip in Boshi Ken. Tori can even hide the right hand from Uke by moving it slightly behind his hip. This

Chi No Kata

Tori stands in Shizen, and Uke is in Ichimonji No Kamae.

43

Uke punches, and Tori steps back into Soshin No Kamaea. Note how it would be possible for Tori to conceal something in his right hand, such as a gun or a knife.

Tori takes Uke's balance by pushing on the inside of Uke's right wrist as he steps in and strikes with a San Shin Tan Ken.

position can also conceal a weapon such as a knife or gun. Once again Uke punches with his right hand towards Tori's face. Tori reacts by stepping back and to the right at 45 degrees with his right leg and blocking Uke's punch with a large circular Jodan Uke, bringing his left arm down to his knee and tracing a semi-circular, anti-clockwise path with his hand until it becomes a fist and blocks Uke's right wrist.

At the same time as Tori is making this blocking movement with his left hand, his right hand should form a fist and come to his forehead. This right hand is held here to guard against another punch or kick. Tori then judges his distance from Uke, draws his left foot back the requisite amount and steps through with his right leg, and aims his right hand in Shuto (*see* the photo on page 25), palm up to Uke's left neck or Uko. Tori should at this point apply some outward pressure to the inside of Uke's wrist to take his balance.

At the same time Tori needs to co-ordinate the straightening of his left leg, the bending of his right knee and the twisting of his body anti-clockwise, thus using his whole body to augment the strike. This technique is very similar to Ichimonji of the Kihon Happo, detailed in the next chapter.

Common Mistakes

Details often omitted are that the Jodan Uke is a strike, and not just a parry. It is aimed to inflict damage with the knuckles of the fist. As Tori steps in, he should push gently on Uke's inside right forearm with his left fist to take some of his balance. The Shuto should be used like a hatchet, and travel from Tori's head straight to its target. A lot of practitioners make the mistake of using a big, circular movement with their arm, but this is too unsubtle and can easily be blocked. The circular motion of the strike

This is how you form the San Shin Tan Ken fist. Also *see* page 90.

should come from the anti-clockwise twisting of Tori's waist. The knees should drive in the direction perpendicular to a line drawn between Uke's feet, to take his balance on impact (*see* page 17). It is vital that Tori captures this complicated movement, as it will enable him to get some power behind his strike.

Ka No Kata (Fire Form)

Uke and Tori face each other as before in Hidari Ichimonji No Kamae and Hidari Soshin No Kamae respectively. Uke punches at Tori's face, and Tori defends as above by stepping back and to the right with his right leg at 45 degrees, sliding his left foot a little out of the way. At the same time Uke does a Jodan Uke to block Uke's punch and, as before, he brings his right fist to his forehead. Tori should then adjust his distance as before, by drawing his left foot back a little and stepping through with his right leg while twisting his body counter clockwise. Tori should then aim his right Shuto directly at Uke's right neck or Uko, while untwisting at the waist in a clockwise direction, and straightening the left leg and pushing the right knee forwards. This all helps to use the body to apply the strike.

Sui No Kata

Uke and Tori assume their respective positions.

As Uke punches, Tori steps back at 45 degrees and does a Jodan Uke block while raising his right hand into a Doko No Kamae to guard.

Sui No Kata *cont.*

Here you can clearly see Tori pushing on the inside of Uke's arm, and his balance is broken.

Tori has adjusted his distance so he can step in and hit Uke with an Omote Shuto, while maintaining an almost straight arm. Tori is still covering Uke's right arm.

Common Mistakes

One of the main points omitted with this technique is not to use the clockwise untwisting of the waist to add force to the strike. This omission seriously diminishes the power that can be developed. Again, Tori should use discreet outward pressure on the inside of Uke's right arm with his left fist to stagger Uke's balance prior to striking.

Fu No Kata (Wind Form)

Once again Uke and Tori face each other in Hidari Ichimonji No Kamae and Hidari Soshin No Kamae respectively. This time Uke punches at Tori's stomach or a Chudan Tsuki. Again Tori steps back and to the right with his right leg and does a large left Gedan Uke – that is, dropping his left hand in a clockwise semi-circular movement to his left knee, and then up to hook Uke's punch in the bend of his wrist, little finger up.

Again Tori adjusts the distance between himself and Uke by bringing his left foot back and stepping through with his right leg. The swap of position from the block to the strike should be quicker than the other techniques, and should have a faster rhythm.

Again by straightening his left back leg and pushing his right knee forwards, Tori should strike with his thumb tip or Boshi Ken (*see* page 25) to Uke's bladder or to the right *koe*, which is the *kyusho* point where the femur joins the hip. This strike should utilize the same pendulum-type swing of Chi No Kata, and Tori should also twist in an anticlockwise direction at the waist and shoulders to add power to the strike. The point of this technique is to use the deceptive range you can achieve, by the use of the dynamic bending of the knees. The correct distancing is found if Tori can hit his target with a near-straight arm.

Ku No Kata (Void Form)

Again, Uke and Tori face each other in Hidari Ichimonji No Kamae and Hidari Soshin No Kamae, and Uke again punches to Tori's stomach. Tori blocks as before by stepping back with his right leg back and to the right at 45 degrees, and does a left Gedan Uke

Ka No Kata

Uke assumes Ichimonji No Kamae, and Tori takes up Soshin No Kamae.

Ka No Kata *cont.*

Tori steps back and to the right, while blocking with a Jodan Uke and raising his right arm to guard.

Tori adjusts his distance and steps in to strike Uke with a Ura Shuto. Note how Tori's body is aligned from his left foot to his right hand.

49

Fu No Kata

Uke and Tori assume their respective positions.

Uke punches to Tori's stomach. Tori steps back and to the right and does a lower block.

Fu No Kata *cont.*

Tori adjusts his distance and steps in and strikes to Uke's bladder with a Boshi Ken.

as described above. Tori then raises his left hand in front of Uke's eyes and up, with his palm facing Uke. This movement acts as a distraction to Uke and momentarily breaks his rhythm and takes his mind to the raised hand. This is called Choshi Dori and translates as taking control of the situation by controlling the timing and rhythm of a fight.

At the same time Tori chambers his right knee to his chest and does a stamping kick to Uke's sternum. The heel should be the striking weapon, and the kick should have the power to break Uke's sternum and knock him over. A trick to get elevation with the kicking leg is for Tori to bend the left supporting leg at the knee. It is also important for him to keep the left foot flat on the ground while kicking and not lift the heel.

Ku No Kata

Uke assumes Ichimonji No Kamae, and Tori takes up Soshin No Kamae.

Ku No Kata *cont.*

Uke punches at Tori's stomach, and Tori does a low block.

Tori raises his right hand, and you can see how it has drawn Uke's attention.

Ku No Kata *cont.*

Tori has chambered his knee to his chest, preparing to kick Uke.

Tori straightening his leg and kicking Uke back.

6 Kihon Happo: Eight Basic Techniques

The Kihon Happo is described as incorporating the basic techniques in the Bujinkan Ninjutsu system. These techniques are far from basic, however, and after eighteen years of studying this particular art, and thirty-two years of studying martial arts in general, I am still learning nuances within the Kihon Happo. As I have mentioned earlier, the previous Grand Master, Takamatsu Toshitsugu, said that the Kihon Happo incorporates the fundamentals of all martial arts.

Hatsumi Sensei has said that 'Ninjutsu is Taijutsu. Taijutsu begins with the Kihon Happo and ends with the Kihon Happo. If you get stuck with technique, go back and redo Kihon Happo.' I have endlessly applied this theory in martial arts training and business. As I have mentioned before, we all have a tendency to over-complicate our lives. We try more and more complicated techniques, and in business we try to expand as quickly as we can, taking on complementary businesses. Sometimes it all stops working. This is the point where you have to go back to the techniques or core businesses that you know fundamentally work. In the case of Ninjutsu it is the Kihon Happo you should go back to.

You should view the Kihon Happo as the roots of a very large tree. If the roots are not strong, the tree will fall over as it starts to grow. The basic principle is to learn the basic eight moves on both left and right side, and then work on *henka*, or variations

of these techniques, as well as applying the techniques in many different directions. Combine this with interlinking of the techniques – for example, combining Musha Dori with Omote Gyaku – and soon you will have an infinite number of variations, or ∞, eight lying on its side, if you like. This also corresponds well with the other interpretation of the words Kihon Happo, which is 'all directional basics'.

Please also consider the fact that there is no right or wrong way to do the techniques, but a basic way and then endless variations that comply with the basic principles. This is contrary to a lot of martial arts that have a rigid structure of doing a technique a certain way, and no other way is acceptable. Each attack is unique in distancing and timing, so each response should, therefore, be unique in its own way. As Hatsumi Sensei has said, if something has a rigid structure, someone or something will come along and break it.

This flexibility should also extend to mindset, and this will enable you to see laterally around different attacks, or problems. It is also possible to be flexible with the way you do technique, and not be a carbon copy of your instructor because your physiology is generally completely different. This is particularly the case with a Japanese instructor and a Western student. This should not become an excuse to do things your own way, however, as the basic principles still need to be adhered to.

When practising the Kihon Happo, it is important to initially break the opponent's *kamae*; this by its nature will also break his balance. Often you can't break the opponent's balance with one move, but you should aim to do it progressively with a series of moves. It is particularly important to consider this when practising *henka*, or variations.

The Kihon Happo is made up of two different parts. The first three techniques are grouped together and called the Kosshi Kihon Sanpo, or three basic ways of Kosshijitsu. The other part is made up of the remaining five techniques and is called the Torite Kihon Kata Goho, or five basic hand-capturing forms.

It is important when training that when the attack is made, it will actually hit its target, and the attacker is not too far away for this to happen. Also the attacker's punch should not track its target – that is, follow the movement of the defender. Practising the Kihon Happo should very much be considered as an opportunity for the attacker to work on his punching and rolling techniques, for example, and not for just the defender to be working on his technique. As mentioned before, you should look at your opponent because you can often pick up his intention to attack through his eyes. This is not a tangible thing, but a feeling you get, and it really helps with your timing.

Kosshi Kihon Sanpo

Ichimonji No Kamae

Attacker (Uke) and defender (Tori) face each other in Hidari Ichimonji No Kamae; they must be the correct distance apart, such that if Uke punches and Tori stays where he is, he will get hit. Uke then punches at Tori's face. Tori steps back with his right leg at 45 degrees and drags his front, left foot back a little, so he is still in posture, but angled away from the attack. At this point Tori's front left

hand drops to his left knee and traces an anti-clockwise, semi-circular path to Uke's wrist; he (Tori) should use his shoulder to do this movement, and not his elbow. To add more power to the block he can rotate his hips anti-clockwise at the point of impact with Uke's right wrist. This movement, as mentioned before, is called Jodan Uke. At the same time Tori's right hand should come up to the forehead with the elbow down to protect the ribs. This position enables Tori to block a second strike, if it were to come, and also disguises the follow-up strike so it is difficult for Uke to determine if it is going to hit the left or the right side of his neck.

Tori should then draw his left foot back a little, while pushing gently on the inside of Uke's right forearm with his left fist to stagger Uke's balance a little. The amount Tori should move his left foot back depends on the physiology of himself and his opponent: it should be such that when he steps forwards with his right leg he is able to hit Uke with a right horizontal Omote Shuto with the arm almost straight. This means the palm of the right hand is up. This right hand should chop from his forehead to the left side of the opponent's neck in a direct fashion. Again, to add power there should be an anti-clockwise twisting from the waist to harness the power of the whole body. At the same time Tori should transfer his weight by driving off his left rear leg and transferring his weight over his right knee. This weight transfer should be in the direction of the perpendicular line illustrated on page 17: this way Tori can strike Uke's neck and drive him backwards off balance at the same time.

Common Mistakes
Common mistakes made with this technique include failure to trace a semi-circular path with the fist, from the knee so you can block punches to the face and below. Also, as mentioned previously, the block is a strike to the

opponent's wrist with the knuckles of the left fist (unlike in many other martial arts, where this movement is just a parry): the hand should be open, and should only clench at the point of impact with the opponent's wrist. Other mistakes include not being on the perpendicular line as depicted on page 17 when you step in with the strike to the neck; and not clenching the right hand and opening it into an Omote Shuto (see page 25) at the point of impact with the opponent's neck. The strike should be horizontal through the neck, much in the same way as you would cut with a sword; it should not cut down into Uke's body.

Hicho No Kamae

For this technique Uke is in Hidari Ichimonji No Kamae and Tori is facing him in Hidari Hicho No Kamae. The same criteria for distancing apply. Uke then punches at Tori's stomach. Tori uses his left hand to trace a clockwise, semi-circular path to his left knee, and up to deflect and catch Uke's wrist with his hooked left wrist. This will, if a mistake is made, help deflect punches from the head down. This movement, as discussed before, is called Chudan Uke; while Tori is making this blocking movement he should raise his right fist to his forehead as with the previous technique.

At the same time Tori should drop his bodyweight by flexing his supporting knee to add power to the block. He should also bend slightly at the waist to make some space between the punch and his stomach. This compressed position leads into the next movement, where Tori expands from the compressed position, hooks Uke's wrist and lifts it up, while at the same time kicking with his left heel to just under Uke's right armpit. Tori should deliver the kick in a stamping fashion, in much the same way that he would kick a door down, by first chambering the left knee to his chest. Tori should then replace his left foot next to his right foot, and step forwards with his right foot, while striking the right side of Uke's neck with a right-handed Ura Shuto – this means with the palm facing downwards. Once again you must use your whole body to deliver the strike, by transferring your weight over your right knee and rotating your waist clockwise to deliver the horizontal chopping strike to the neck.

Common Mistakes

Common mistakes made with this technique include failure to compress the body downwards when blocking the punch, and not expanding the body upwards when kicking. Other details that the student needs to be aware of are to control the opponent's right arm from the moment it is blocked, so it can't be used to strike again. With this contact with his right arm you can feel the subtle changes in his balance, which will telegraph any intention Uke has of trying another attack.

Jumonji No Kamae

Uke and Tori face each other. Tori is in Hidari Jumonji No Kamae and Uke is in Hidari Ichimonji No Kamae. Uke punches to Tori's face. Tori steps back and to the right with his right leg to move out of the way of the punch, and also drops his weight. He then uses a *small* semi-circular, anti-clockwise movement of his left arm to hit Uke's right arm, just under the elbow with his left fist. This movement is also called Jodan Uke. Tori then rocks forwards over his left knee as he strikes Uke into his right armpit with a left Boshi Ken (see page 25); this action is very much like a lunge in fencing, and Tori can augment his power by driving off his back, right leg.

Tori then rakes his left fingers in front of Uke's eyes, at which point Uke steps and punches with his left fist to Tori's face. Tori steps back and to the left with his left foot, and does the same type of block as before, but this time with his right fist on to Uke's

Ichimonji No Kamae

Tori and Uke face each other in Ichimonji No Kamae.

As Uke punches at Tori, he does a Jodan Uke block and raises his right arm to a Doko position as a guard.

Ichimonji No Kamae *cont.*

Tori then adjusts his distance and steps in and hits Uke with an Omote Shuto. Note how Tori's arm is almost straight.

Hicho No Kamae

Uke and Tori face each other. This time Tori is in Hicho No Kamae.

Hicho No Kamae *cont.*

Uke punches to Tori's stomach. Note how Tori has blocked, and is also in a compressed position and is guarding against another attack.

Tori then kicks to an area under Uke's armpit with his heel.

Hicho No Kamae *cont.*

Tori then controls Uke's right arm as he steps in and strikes Uke's neck with a Ura Shuto.

Tori contols Uke's arm in a lock, and pulls his head down. Also note how Tori is controlling Uke's right foot.

Jumonji No Kamae

Tori and Uke face each other. This time Tori is in Jumonji No Kamae.

Tori moves back at 45 degrees and blocks Uke's right punch just under his elbow.

Jumonji No Kamae *cont.*

Tori then rocks in by transferring his weight over his left leg to strike Uke's armpit with a Boshi Ken.

Tori then moves his left hand in front of Uke's eyes.

Jumonji No Kamae *cont*.

Uke punches with his left fist. Tori steps back and to the left while blocking with his right fist under Uke's elbow.

Tori, without stepping, transfers his weight over his right knee to strike Uke's armpit with Boshi Ken.

Jumonji No Kamae *cont.*

Tori runs his right fingers in front of Uke's eyes.

Tori then steps back into Kosei No Kamae to observe Uke's next move.

left elbow. He once again uses the previous weight transfer, this time over his right knee, and strikes with a right Boshi Ken to Uke's left armpit. He rakes his right fingers in front of Uke's eyes and then steps back with his right leg and assumes Hidari Kosei No Kamae to observe Uke's next move.

Common Mistakes
Common mistakes that are made while doing this technique include using the blocking movement of the arms to avoid the punches, and not the movement of the body using footwork. This blocking movement should mainly be done with the shoulders, as discussed. Another common mistake is to move too far back with the evasive footwork, making it necessary to step forwards to strike. The striking movement should just come from the weight transfer over the front knee, with no superfluous stepping. Another small detail is that, once the opponent's elbow is struck, Tori should run his fist along Uke's upper arm to control it, so it does not become a danger again, and swing towards Tori's face.

Torite Kihon Kata Goho

Omote Gyaku (Outside Twist)
Uke and Tori face each other while standing in Shizen No Kamae, and Uke grabs Tori's left lapel with his right hand. Tori rests his left palm against Uke's fist with his fingers on top. It is important that Tori does not go to grab Uke's hand, as this will signify the beginning of a technique and Uke consequently will become wary. Tori should then step back and to the right with his right leg, while at the same time controlling Uke's right elbow with his left elbow, and lowering his hips. This movement should make Uke step forwards as his balance has been broken.

Tori should cover a potential left punch from Uke with his right hand as he moves his right hand in front of Uke and across Uke's eyes to Uke's right hand. Tori should then hold Uke's right hand with both his hands and push Uke's hand vertically up and off his lapel, while raising his body up a little, pushing in with the tips of both thumbs into the nerve point or *kyusho* in the middle of the back of Uke's hand. Tori should then step back and to the left with his left leg while pushing Uke's right palm towards Uke's forearm and rotating Uke's hand anti-clockwise, and at the same time taking Uke's right hand to his left knee. Uke should apply a backward roll to avoid injury.

Common Mistakes
Common mistakes made with this technique are for Tori to grab Uke's hand too hard at the start of the technique and warn Uke of a pending technique. Another mistake is for Tori not to control Uke's right elbow with his left elbow midway through the technique. Tori can use this control to help take Uke's hand off the lapel or, if he tries to punch with the left hand, Tori can lock Uke's elbow out, so he can't get close enough to hit him. Tori can also use this elbow control to straighten Uke's arm, which is a good way to apply this technique. It is important to control the space between Uke and Tori. This is done with the covering right hand.

Another common mistake is for Tori not to fold Uke's hand in towards his forearm before twisting, and also failing to use a pulling movement to augment the wrist twist. This pulling movement stops Uke regaining his balance, thus making it impossible to resist the lock. It also straightens Uke's arm, which is an important feature of this technique. One other mistake is for Tori to try and apply these wrist twists with straight arms. For reasons of leverage it is better to keep your hands close to your body and Uke's hand away from his body.

65

Omote Gyaku Tsuki (Outside Twist with Punch)

As above, both Uke and Tori are facing each other in Shizen No Kamae. Uke grabs Tori's left lapel with his right hand, and steps and punches to Tori's face with his left side. Tori guards Uke's grabbing hand gently as before, and as Uke punches, he steps back and to the left with his left leg while lowering his position. At the same time Uke does a right Jodan Uke and blocks the punch in a fashion similar to the Jumonji block: this has a smaller rotation of the arm before the fist hits into the nerve point right above and underneath Uke's left elbow. Tori's hands then move in front of Uke's eyes as they move to hold Uke's right hand, lifting it up and then pulling it to Tori's left knee while applying the Omote Gyaku wrist twist. Tori can also step forwards with his right leg and back with his left leg to help apply the twist.

Common Mistakes

One mistake often made is not getting low enough when blocking Uke's punch. Tori should apply the Omote Gyaku to Uke's wrist and then drag it using weight transfer to his left knee, not the strength in his arms. Another point is for Tori to guard against potential kicks. If Tori feels Uke building up for a kick at any point, he can push down on Uke's left hand so it pulls Uke forwards and down to block any chance of him lifting a foot to kick; or if a kick is initiated, Uke will have to place his foot back on the ground immediately to regain his balance. Tori should also use his right arm, once it has blocked Uke's punch, to fill the space between the two of them. This is a high-level principle of Tori filling the space between him and Uke, to block Uke from using it. This effectively gives Tori control of this space, or *kukan*, to use it as he wishes.

Ura Gyaku (Inside Twist)

Uke and Tori face each other in Shizen No Kamae. Uke grabs Tori's left lapel with his right hand. Tori gently holds Uke's hand with his left hand as before. Tori steps back and to the left with his left leg to stagger Uke's balance. Tori then moves his right hand in front of Uke's eyes while covering a potential left punch, again controlling the *kukan*. Tori reaches over Uke's right hand and pushes his right thumb into the space between Uke's right thumb and forefinger, and grips the bottom of Uke's hand with his fingers, with his palm against the back of Uke's hand. It is really important for Tori to get this strong grip on Uke's hand. Tori then turns Uke's hand, little finger up. He then rotates his upper body clockwise to apply pressure to the back of Uke's hand with his chest, to push the palm towards Uke's forearm and augment the twist on Uke's wrist.

Once Tori has this position he holds Uke's right hand with both hands and pushes Uke's fingers forwards and down as he walks forwards: this will throw Uke forwards into a forward break fall. Tori can make this technique stronger by pushing up on Uke's slightly bent right elbow with his left hand; he can also apply a variation called Hon Gyaku, where he rotates Uke's hand, fingers backwards, so they are pointing at Tori, then with his left hand he pushes down on Uke's bent elbow, while trying to push Uke's little finger towards his nose. This causes immense pressure on Uke's wrist and can cause his knees to buckle.

Common Mistakes

A mistake often made in this technique is for Tori to fail to get a strong enough grip on Uke's hand prior to applying the technique, consequently allowing Uke to slip out of the lock. Another mistake is for Tori to be too static, and when doing the first two variations to fail to walk with the technique

Omote Gyaku

Uke and Tori face each other in Shizen No Kamae.

Uke grabs Tori's collar, and Tori gently covers Uke's hand.

Tori steps back and to the right with his right leg and controls Uke's elbow with his elbow. This makes it difficult for Uke to attack with his other hand.

Omote Gyaku *cont.*

Close-up of Tori's hand grip on Uke's hand.

Left: Tori holds Uke's hand with both hands and pushes it up, using his arms and body.

Tori pushes Uke's hand inwards towards Uke's forearm, and steps back and to the left with his left leg. At the same time Tori twists Uke's wrist anti-clockwise, while keeping Uke's arm straight.

Omote Gyaku Tsuki

Uke and Tori face each other in Shizen No Kamae, and Uke grabs Tori's collar.

Below: Uke punches with his left hand. Tori covers Uke's hand, and steps back and to the left with his left leg while striking up under Uke's elbow.

Omote Gyaku Tsuki *cont.*

Tori applies Omote Gyaku. Note how Tori keeps his hands close to his body while extending Uke's arm.

so as to avoid reaching and putting himself off balance. This walking principle is very important on two counts: firstly, so that Tori does not sacrifice his own balance if his range of movement is not sufficient to make the technique work – if Tori needs a larger range of movement he should use his footwork to obtain this. And secondly, if Tori is walking and moving he becomes a much harder target for other opponents, apart from Uke, to hit. In this example I am thinking of Uke's friends.

Musha Dori (Capture a Warrior)
Uke and Tori face each other and hold each other in Shizen No Kamae. Uke and Tori then grab each other's right sleeve with their left hand and each other's left lapel with their right hand. This hold is called Kumiuchi. Tori steps back and to the right with his right leg, pulling Uke and making him make a

step forwards with his left leg. Tori then steps back in with his right leg while turning his right hand thumb down and using it to press gently on Uke's left elbow to make it bend slightly. As Uke's elbow bends, Tori lowers his position and his footwork makes his body rotate anti-clockwise so that he is facing in the same direction as Uke's shoulders, so they are parallel.

Tori then rises up a little while making a fist with his right hand and cupping it with his left hand: he uses it to lift Uke's elbow up to lock it. Uke's left wrist should be trapped under Tori's right armpit. Tori then stamps to the *kyusho* at the back of Uke's left knee, on the top of Uke's calf, with his right foot, toes pointing outwards. This will break Uke's balance, and Tori should immediately step back with his right leg and kneel on it, to take Uke to the floor. Tori can step over Uke's body with his left leg and pin him

70

Ura Gyaku

Uke grabs Tori's collar, and Tori covers Uke's hand gently.

Tori steps back and to the left with his left leg still covering Uke's right hand. Note how Tori covers a potential attack from Uke's left hand.

Tori reaches over with his right hand and grabs Uke's hand.

71

Ura Gyaku *cont.*

Close-up of Tori's grip on Uke's hand. It is important that this is a strong grip.

Left: Tori turns clockwise, and you can see how he uses his chest to twist Uke's wrist.

Ura Gyaku *cont.*

Uke walks forwards while twisting Uke's wrist.
This will force Uke to roll forwards.

while continuing with the upward pressure on his elbow, to break the shoulder joint or gain a submission. Another control is for Tori to kneel on Uke's neck with his right knee.

Common Mistakes
A common mistake made with this technique is for Tori not to turn enough to ensure that his shoulders are parallel with Uke's. Tori can use his left hand in front of Uke's face to control the *kukan*. Another mistake is for Tori to interlace his fingers once he has the lock.

Ganseki Nage (Throw a Rock)
This technique takes a while to perfect, and practice is the key here. Uke and Tori start facing each other in Shizen No Kamae. They then grab each other's right sleeve with their left hand, and each other's left lapel with their right hand, called Kumiuchi. Tori responds

as before by stepping back and to the right with his right leg to stagger Uke's balance. Tori can also control the space between them by holding his left arm on the inside of Uke's right arm.

Tori should then step between his opponent's legs with his right foot, while driving his right arm under Uke's armpit to the outside of Uke's shoulder, with his hand up. This should break Uke's grip on Tori's sleeve, and allow Uke's wrist to move up behind Tori's neck. Tori should arch his head back to trap Uke's left wrist in this position.

Tori should then step back and around with his left leg, while making a shot-putting movement with his right arm, making sure his arm is pressing against Uke's elbow. At the same time he should rotate his body anticlockwise. This movement will lock Uke's elbow and force him to be thrown.

73

Musha Dori

Uke and Tori hold each other in a Judo-style grip.

Below: Tori steps back and to the right with his right leg, while controlling both of Uke's elbows.

Musha Dori *cont.*

Tori captures Uke's elbow in Musha Dori. Note how Tori has completely taken Uke's balance while maintaining his own.

Common Mistakes

One common mistake is for Tori not to hook Uke's wrist with the back of his neck, allowing Uke's arm to escape. Another mistake is that Tori allows his right hand to drop while throwing Uke, which takes away some of the effectiveness as it destroys Tori's posture and alignment; Tori should use a shot-putting type of movement. The other mistake is to fail to circle the left leg back and around prior to throwing. This technique is one of the hardest to perfect, and as mentioned earlier requires a lot of practice.

An interesting exercise to try with the last two techniques is to manipulate the techniques from the same grips and positions, but on the opponent's other arm.

In Summary

In the last two chapters of techniques I have progressively added more details and concepts from one technique to the next; this is why there are certain elements that in places are repeated. The descriptions have been written this way intentionally, however, to help the reader internalize the moves, and also so as not to overload the practitioner with too many ideas in the first few techniques, but adding more detail as the reader progressively develops.

Ganseki Nage

Tori and Uke hold each other in a judo-type grip.

Tori circles his arm under Uke's armpit.

Tori steps in front of Uke and locks his arm behind his head. Note how Tori's arm points upwards.

Ganseki Nage *cont.*

Tori assumes the Ganseki position, and can control Uke's right arm if desired. Note how Uke's left leg is also locked, which is a bonus.

Tori transfers his weight over his left leg as he turns to his left. Note how Tori's left arm is still kept high.

7 Additional Techniques

The next three techniques are not strictly part of the Kihon Happo; however, they perfectly complement it. They are basically a series of elbow and shoulder locks, which will add to the serious martial artist's repertoire. As always the principle of taking the opponent's balance first, and then applying the technique, should be applied.

Omote Oni Kudaki (Outer Version of Destroying a Devil)

Both Uke and Tori hold each other's right sleeve with their left hand, and each other's left lapel with their right hand. Tori then steps back at 45 degrees with his left leg as he covers the inside of Uke's right wrist with the back of his left wrist. Tori then steps in with his right leg, and moves his right arm behind Uke's right arm and joins hands by holding the fingers of his left hand with his right hand. While keeping Uke's arm close to his chest Tori takes a half step back with his right leg, and while pressing down on Uke's right wrist and up on his right elbow, Tori steps back with his left leg, throwing Uke to the ground.

Common Mistakes
Common mistakes made with this technique are not to make the hand grip correctly, to trap Uke's wrist. I have seen a lot of people omit the half step back with the right leg, and this stops the lock being as strong as it could

be. Also the raising of Uke's elbow while at the same time lowering his wrist are often poorly handled.

Omote Oni Kudaki

Tori and Uke hold each other with a Judo-style grip.

78

Omote Oni Kudaki cont.

Tori takes Uke's balance by stepping back with his left leg. To attack Uke further, Tori can use a right Boshi Ken into Uke's throat.

Tori then steps in with his right knee, and you can see him controlling Uke's right knee. Also Tori's left hand has moved to the inside of Uke's right wrist.

Omote Oni Kudaki *cont.*

This is the close-up of the control. Note how Tori's hand is bent back to hook Uke's wrist.

Tori has now stepped back with his right foot and is lifting with his right elbow and dropping his hands to apply the lock.

Omote Oni Kudaki *cont.*

Now Tori has stepped back with his left leg and increases the pressure of the lock. He is aiming to impact Uke against the wall and ground.

Uke managed to avoid hitting the wall when he was thrown down. Tori assumes a posture to see what kind of threat Uke continues to be.

Ura Oni Kudaki (Inner Version of Destroying a Devil)

Uke and Tori face each other in Shizen No Kamae. Uke and Tori then grab each other's right sleeve with their left hand and each other's left lapel with their right hand. Again, Tori should step back at 45 degrees with his left leg, causing Uke to step forward with his right leg. Tori should then step in with his right leg and reach over Uke's right arm with his right arm, and hook Uke's elbow to his chest with the thumb side of his wrist. This movement will help to bend Uke's elbow. At the same time Tori should hold Uke's right wrist from the inside, with his left hand. Tori then steps forward with his left leg, while raising Uke's right elbow and pushing his right wrist down, to throw him backwards and down.

Some Pointers

Some pointers for this technique are to try to keep Uke's lower arm, upper arm and his side of the body all at 90 degrees in relation to each other. This bit of advice is useful for the previous technique as well. It is also important to keep Uke's elbow hooked to Tori's chest.

Muso Dori (Catching a Strong Man)

Both Uke and Tori hold each other's right sleeve with their left hand, and each other's left lapel with their right hand. Tori then steps back and to the left with his left leg, making Uke step with his right leg. Tori should then step in with his left leg, while circling his right leg back so his shoulders are parallel with Uke's. At the same time Tori circles his left hand from the inside to the outside of Uke's right arm, and cups Uke's point of the elbow, making sure it points upwards, with

Ura Oni Kudaki

Again Tori and Uke face each other and take a Judo-style grip.

his left hand. This movement should also ensure that Uke's right wrist is caught in the bend of Tori's left elbow. Now Tori can push down on the point of Uke's elbow and lift with his own left elbow, to over-extend Uke's elbow joint, while at the same time walking forwards in the direction shown in the illustration on page 17 to force Uke face down to the ground.

Tori can control Uke on the ground by kneeling on his right shoulder blade with his

Ura Oni Kudaki *cont.*

Tori steps back with his left leg and moves his left hand to the inside of Uke's right wrist.

Tori steps in with his right leg and wraps Uke's right arm. Tori could also take the opportunity to strike Uke's chin with his right elbow at this point.

Ura Oni Kudaki *cont.*

This is a close-up of Tori's control on Uke's arm. Tori should try and keep all parts of Uke's arm at 90 degrees to each other.

left knee and pushing Uke's right arm backwards, over his own shoulder with his hips, to lock the shoulder joint. Tori should make sure Uke's chest is flat on the ground, so as to have good control.

As with all techniques, the Henka or variations should also be practised. An easy Henka is to try to apply the technique on the opponent's other arm while still using the principles of Tai Jutsu.

Tori has transferred his weight over his left leg, but is still controlling Uke's left leg with his right leg. Again Tori is aiming to impact Uke against the wall.

Muso Dori

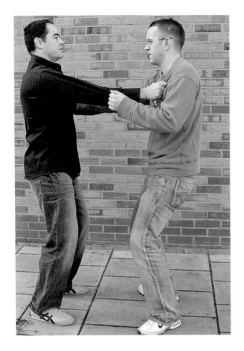

Uke and Tori hold each other with Judo-style grips.

Tori steps back with his left leg to take Uke's balance, and controls Uke's right elbow with his left hand.

Tori rotates Uke's elbow so the point is up. Note how Tori is also looking to see what is going on, so as not to be taken by surprise by another opponent.

Muso Dori *cont.*

Tori has now stepped in with his left foot, and note how it is controlling Uke's right foot. Tori is also applying pressure to Uke's elbow joint, making Uke bend at the waist.

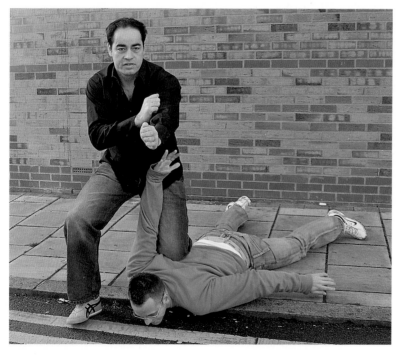

Tori has taken Uke to the ground and is pinning him with a shoulder lock. Note how Tori is in posture in case there is another opponent. Also Tori has been aware of the curb and negotiated it without stumbling.

8 Hoken Juroppo (Sixteen Secret Fists)

These are the sixteen secret body weapons used for striking in the Ninjutsu system; some of these are very specific for soft or hard targets. The weapons used on soft tissue tend to be of a small surface area so as to penetrate the opponent's body or find a small specific pressure point; they are therefore small-boned, delicate and fragile if used against harder areas. The weapons used against harder body targets are thicker and more robust so as not to be damaged when used; their surface area is also larger, and therefore less useful at getting into, or hitting specific points. If you wish to train all these weapons, you should start with a soft striking surface, and over time make it harder. However, it is no longer appropriate to have damaged, over-conditioned hands and feet, as nowadays we also have to have dexterity. Furthermore, hands like this make it easy for people to see that you are a martial artist, and this may not always be desired.

Kikaku Ken (Demon Horn Fist)

This technique uses the back, sides and particularly the thick-boned area of the forehead, also the corners of the forehead, to strike the opponent. If power is to be transferred with a forehead strike it is very important to align the neck with the rest of the spine, so as not to damage it. I have also been taught to shrug the shoulders to help support the neck area.

As always, it is important to get the body behind the strike.

Here is an example of using the forehead: if Uke punches with a right fist, Tori should do a left Jodan Uke and then charge in like a bull to strike Uke's right Butsumetsu, or the side of his ribcage. Tori should easily be able to develop enough power to break Uke's ribs.

Kikaku Ken

Note how I am shrugging my shoulders to help support my neck; also how I have aligned my neck, so as not to damage it.

Shuki Ken (Waking Up Arm Fist)

This is using the bony point of the elbow to strike the opponent. It can be used in a circular horizontal motion, backwards and forwards, as well as in a vertical plane, up and down. It is also possible to use the point of the elbow as a battering ram against the opponent's chest. The elbow is the perfect weapon to use when bridging the distance between punching and grappling, and it is also one of the most powerful weapons available to the unarmed human.

Here is an example of the use of the elbow: if Uke punches with a right punch to Tori's face, Tori steps back and to the right with his right leg, and does a left Jodan Uke to Uke's right wrist. Tori steps in and punches Uke in the solar plexus with his right fist. This strike will cause Uke's chin to peck forwards, exposing it to a vertical elbow strike from low to high.

Fudo Ken (Immovable Fist)

A fist is made by clenching the fingers as tight as possible into the palm of the hand: aim to make the fist tight enough so the fingernails are not visible; the thumb should run down the side of the fingers. The striking surface is the four base knuckles of the hand. It is not ideal to use this type of fist to hit a hard target such as the opponent's face, as the hand is easily broken – as many boxers have proved to their cost when fighting outside the ring. It is also possible to use just the knuckles of the fore and middle fingers. To get into small specific pressure points the knuckle of the little finger can be used. When punching above shoulder height, or anywhere near this height, it is wise to rotate the fist so the thumb is upwards, so as not to over-stress the wrist by having the hand forced down on impact. For this reason in Ninjutsu this is always the favoured position to punch.

If Uke punches with a right punch to Tori's face, Tori steps back and to the right with his right leg, and at the same time performs a

Shuki Ken

The point of the elbow.

Fudo Ken

This is how to form the regular fist.

Jodan Uke. Tori should then step in with his right leg, and strike Uke's solar plexus with a right Fudo Ken. As Uke's chin pecks forwards, Tori should run the right Fudo Ken up Uke's sternum, at the same time arching back with his spine to hit Uke under the chin. If done correctly, Uke should not see this second punch.

Kiten Ken aka Shuto Ken (Get Up and Fall Down Fist)

This fist has been discussed earlier in the book, but I will detail it again to keep this section complete. The striking hand should be folded at the base knuckles, to an angle of 60–90 degrees. The striking area is the bony section on the little finger side of the hand, just above the wrist. The hand can be made more rigid by pressing down with the thumb. The strike can be made with the palm up or down: Omote and Ura Shuto. 'Shu' translates as 'hand' and 'To' means 'sword', together meaning 'sword hand' – so the edge of the hand should be used like a sword.

This is an example of the use of this fist: Uke punches with his left fist to Tori's face. Tori steps back and to the left with his left leg, and does a right Jodan Uke to Uke's wrist. Tori then takes a step in with his left leg, while hitting with a left Omote Shuto to the same point on Uke's wrist. Then Tori takes a small step forwards with his left leg while hitting horizontally to the left side of Uke's neck with a Ura Shuto.

Shishin Ken (Finger Needle Fist)

This uses the little finger, and clearly it should be used against soft delicate targets such as the eyes and specific *kyusho* as the little finger is easily damaged. I remember being at a Tai Kai when Hatsumi Sensei demonstrated the use of this weapon on me. Basically he pushed his little finger into my ear canal and found a *kyusho* point inside the canal. I remember it had me on tip toes, and I felt as if I were being electrocuted through my whole body.

Kiten Ken

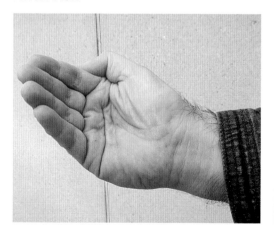

The fingers should be bent, and the thumb presses down to make the hand more rigid. The striking area is the edge of the hand, just above the wrist.

Shishin Ken

The little finger.

Here is one way of using Shishin Ken: if Uke punches with his right fist to Tori's face, Tori should step back and to the left with his left leg, and do a right Jodan Uke. Then if he steps with his left leg, he is able to get behind Uke. Tori can then grab Uke's face and use his little fingers to attack the corners of Uke's mouth.

Shitan Ken (Finger Tip Fist)

This fist has also been discussed previously and is also called San Shin Tan Ken, but again to keep this section complete, I will give details here as well. This fist is made by holding the little finger and thumb together, then squeezing the tips of the ring finger and forefinger together, and reinforcing these two fingers with the tip of the middle finger. This fist, because of the small surface area it presents, is ideal for hitting small targets such as the eyes and *kyusho*.

Here is an example of how to use this fist: Uke punches with his left fist to Tori's face; Tori steps back at 45 degrees with his left leg and performs a right Jodan Uke to Uke's left arm. Tori steps in with his left leg and

circles his right leg back as he strikes with left Shitan Ken to Uke's right temple. The circling of Tori's right leg backwards helps to get the whole body behind the strike.

Shako Ken (Claw Fist)

This uses the hand as a claw, with the fingertips and nails tearing or scratching the opponent's flesh like a wild animal, and the heel of the palm to strike. Shako Ken is ideal for attacking the opponent's face, where you can tear at the delicate skin tissue with the fingertips and also strike the nose with the heel of the palm. The Shako Ken can also be used to grab the flesh and muscle under the opponent's armpit if they are not wearing a suitable jacket. You can also use this fist to grab the opponent's ears, and even the clavicle.

Here is an example of using this technique: Tori avoids a left punch to the face from Uke with a right Jodan Uke, and steps back and to the left with his left leg. Then Tori should step in with his left leg and grab Uke's throat with his left Shako Ken. To do this technique properly you should grip right behind the windpipe.

Shitan Ken

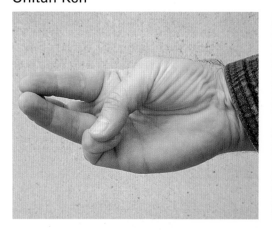

Strike using the tips of the fingers.

Shako Ken

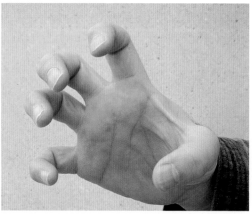

Rake using the nails and finger tips.

Shito Ken aka Boshi Ken (Finger Sword Fist)

I have mentioned this hand form earlier. This hand weapon is made by clenching the fist and resting the extended thumb on top of the forefinger. The striking area is the tip of the thumb, and should be used in a stabbing motion with the whole body behind the strike. Again this weapon should be used against soft tissue areas and should only have the very tip unsupported by the forefinger, as the joint of the thumb can be easily damaged. It can be used to strike points such as the facial nerve, the throat, under the armpit, the joint where the femur joins the hip, and the bladder, to name but a few.

Here is an example of how to use Boshi Ken: Uke punches at Tori's stomach with his right fist. Tori steps back and to the right with his right leg, and performs a left Gedan Uke. Tori adjusts the distance and then steps in with his left leg, and strikes to Uke's side with a left Boshi Ken, driving the thumb between the ribs. To add further discomfort Tori can twist his thumb clockwise to force the ribs apart. As you can imagine, this is extremely painful.

Shito Ken

Strike using the tip of the thumb.

Shikan Ken

The stiking area is the extended knuckles

Shikan Ken (Extended Knuckle Fist)

This fist is made by folding the fingers at the second knuckle and using this edge of the second knuckles to strike with. This fist can be used to strike with, as well as in a slashing motion. You can use this fist to hit slightly harder targets, such as the top lip, the throat, the sternum, and with a slashing motion across the bridge of the nose.

Here is an example of the use of this fist: Uke punches to Tori's face with his left fist. Tori steps back and to the left with his left leg, and performs a right Jodan Uke. Tori then steps in with his right leg and strikes with a right Shikan Ken to Uke's left cheek, hitting the facial nerve.

Koppo Ken (Main Knuckle Fist)

To make this fist you should make a tight fist and then put your thumb on top of your forefinger. This will cause the knuckle of the thumb to protrude, and this is the striking surface you should use. Again you can use this weapon to hit slightly harder targets such as the temple, the sides of the

Koppo Ken

Strike using the raised knuckle of the thumb.

Happa Ken

Use the hands in this cupped position to strike with the palms.

ribs, the kidneys, and the *kyusho* on the thighs.

When Uke punches with a right fist to Tori's face, Tori should step away and to the right with his right leg and perform a left Jodan Uke. Tori should then step in with his right leg as he strikes with both Koppo Kens to both sides of Uke's neck. Alternatively as Tori steps in with his right leg, he grabs Uke's right collar with his left hand and Uke's left collar with his right, fingers in and little fingers upwards. Tori can then roll both his Koppo Kens into Uke's neck. This action will generate extreme pressure and potentially occlude the carotid artery and jugular vein, causing unconsciousness within approximately ten seconds.

Happa Ken (Eight Leaves Fist)

This uses the cupped hand or hands, and is mainly directed against the ears. Extreme care should be taken when using this fist, as it is very easy to blow out the opponent's ear drums. This will clearly cause deafness, but may also upset the opponent's balance as the inner ear is easily damaged.

Here is an example of this weapon: Uke punches with a right punch at Tori's face. Tori steps back and to the right with his right leg while performing a left Jodan Uke. Tori then steps in with his right leg and slaps Uke's ears with both Happa Kens; Tori then immediately turns his hands into Koppo Ken and strikes to both of Uke's temples.

Sokuyaku Ken (Dancing Foot Fist)

This technique uses the sole of the foot for striking: it can be either edge of the foot, the heel of the foot and the ball of the foot. This is a very strong strike and can deliver devastating knock-down power with good range. The sides of the foot can be used to parry the opponent's kicks as well as punches. If you turn your foot with the sole inwards and big toe up, you can use the inside edge of the foot to strike the opponent's groin as the foot now has a narrower profile. The heel is good for delivering maximum power and will easily break the opponent's bones. The ball of the foot will deliver nearly the same power, but has slightly a longer range.

Sokuyaku Ken

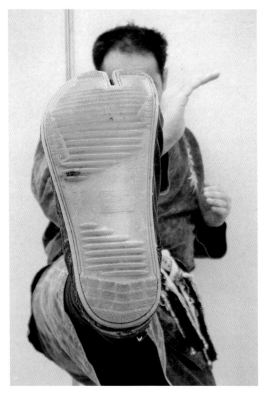

Strike with the heel and the sole of the foot.
You can also use the ball of the foot.

Sokki Ken

Here is the strongest weapon, the knee.

Here is an example of the use of this fist: Uke punches with a left punch to Tori's face, and Tori does a crescent kick with his right foot using the outside of his right foot to parry Uke's punch. Tori then chambers his right knee to his chest and does a stamping kick to Uke's sternum. This kick should easily have enough power to break Uke's sternum and knock him off his feet.

Sokki Ken (Waking Up Leg Fist)

This is the use of the point of the knee to strike, and is the most powerful of the human's weapons. It is only limited by its range. It is ideal for using when you are closing the distance on your opponent, or are moving in to grapple. The combination of the elbow and knee is very powerful, and these weapons are perfect for close range fighting. The knee is very good for attacking the *kyusho* of the opponent's thigh, also his solar plexus, sternum and face.

Here is an example of how to use the Sokki Ken: Uke punches at Tori's face with his left fist, Tori steps back and to the left with his left leg. Tori should then step in with his left leg, and with both Shako Ken grab both of Uke's ears. Then by lowering his posture, Tori should bring Uke's head down as he

93

Sokugyaku Ken

Use the tips of the toes as a weapon. Against soft tissue, this hurts.

Tai Ken

This is an example of using the shoulder as a ram.

strikes upwards to Uke's face with a right Sokki Ken.

Sokugyaku Ken (Toe Reverse Fist)

This weapon involves the use of the tips of the toes, which allows you to get into small *kyusho* points and soft tissue targets. Obviously due to the relatively delicate nature of the toes and the power of the legs, care must be taken when hitting firmer targets as it is easy to damage the toes with the power available from the legs. The feet and legs should be trained to such a level that they have the dexterity of the arms and hands and are able

to perform many of the tasks the hands can, such as striking small *kyusho* points with finesse.

You can use one foot, or you can jump up and strike with both feet at the same time to targets such as the diaphragm. To do this, you have to jump up and drive, up and underneath the ribcage with the toes. With a strike like this it is possible to interrupt the opponent's breathing, and in extreme cases, damage the opponent's heart, potentially causing death. Other areas to strike with this weapon are under the nose, the throat and the armpits, for example.

Here is an example of the use of this weapon: if Uke punches with a right punch to Tori's face, Tori would step back at 45 degrees with his right leg and perform a left Jodan Uke block to Uke's right wrist. Tori should then kick to Uke's throat with a right Sokugyaku Ken.

Tai Ken (Body Fist)

This is the use of the body, namely the hips and the shoulders, as a weapon. This is done by ramming the opponent with your body. Because of the size of these weapons they are used more as a battering ram-type weapon. The use of the shoulder against the opponent's ribcage is very effective at breaking the ribs and knocking the opponent over. The most important point is to use the whole body behind the strike.

Here is an example of how to use this strike: Uke bear-hugs Tori over his arms. Tori should drop his weight and strike with the back of his head to Uke's face, and at the same time strike to Uke's groin with his buttocks. Tori should then raise both his arms and slip under one of Uke's arms and apply Ura Gyaku to the wrist.

Shizen Ken (Natural Fist)

This is the use of natural weapons such as the teeth and nails to bite and scratch. These sorts of weapon are obviously used at very close range, when grappling for example. Most areas of the opponent's body are susceptible to being bitten or scratched.

An example of this fist is, if Tori is grappling with Uke on the ground, this would be a time for Tori to either scratch or bite Uke.

Shizen Ken

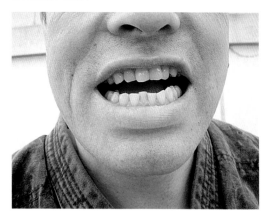

Here are the teeth, for biting.

95

9 Training Pointers

Below is some of my own training advice, and tips to help the student progress. Some of the topics have been mentioned earlier in this book, but introducing further concepts only now was intentional, so as not to overload the student in the first instance.

Form

The Kihon Happo and San Shin No Kata are concepts in movement and shouldn't be overdrilled. When a technique is drilled too much it can become too ingrained, which is all very well, but can be to the detriment of creativity and mental flexibility. It can result in the practitioner considering these same techniques to be the primary solution, and this prevents his transition to other variations. My students will repeat a specific technique five or six times, and then we move to a new technique. This gives the student the feeling of the technique, where form has limits, feelings are unlimited. This is the style of teaching in Japan, and eventually the practitioner will find that he can respond freely to attacks without considering only the basic moves from the Katas. So it is important to be able to break the form. However, to be able to break the form, you really need to know and understand it – and this is the paradox that besets the skilled martial artist. In a way, the form should be considered as a prompt for many possibilities.

Striking

Something else that should be practised regularly is actually hitting something, such as a heavy punchbag or a hand-held bag. This is really important in order to hone your punching and kicking techniques, as it gives you the feeling of actually moving something with a similar mass to a human's body. Without this type of training the drilling of punching and kicking is good, but without the bag-work it becomes rather academic. You should use all the different hand forms you would strike with in order to condition your hands, and you should do the same with your feet and the other body weapons.

Kyo Jitsu Tenkan (the Weaving of Truth and Falsehood)

This is the method of switching truth and falsehood or deception in lay terms, presenting things that look true but are actually false, and vice versa. An example of this is how you use your *kamae*. By leaning forwards from the waist you can give your opponent the impression you are closer than you actually are, and encourage him to attack you; like this you effectively take control of the situation, and make him do something that perhaps he wouldn't otherwise have done. For a deception to be believable there needs to be an element of truth about it, and for a feint to be effective it has to appear to be a real attack and not just a feeble attempt that will be ignored by your enemy. If you want a lie to be believed, likewise it is also wise to interweave the lie with details of truth.

There is also the issue of not looking powerful, even though you are well trained. If you strut around as a 'big game', you will eventually draw a better big game hunter, who will want your head as a 'trophy'. Surely it is much better to move unseen and quietly go about your business. These sort of people, who present themselves as big and powerful, will be the first to be killed in a time of war, or in our current time, during a terrorist hostage situation for example.

Because the practitioner should have a clear, balanced perspective and perception, they should be able to dabble with this falsehood aspect without being corrupted or drawn into a dark realm of untruths, and then find their way back unaided to the white light of truth. Clearly the use of deception should not be used for any bad causes, but as a means of achieving an honest goal. Deception should be a means and not the end. If you regularly tell lies, you will not be believed by others in the end, so the act becomes pointless. You will also get lost yourself in what is true and what is false, which is also self-defeating. Also, as I have mentioned previously, please be aware that one of the points of Ninjutsu is to forge a true and honest heart, and the telling of lies will not help in this pursuit.

With regard to technique, it is important not to show the opponent, or more importantly let him feel what you are doing or are going to do, until he is trapped. If you approach your opponent and handle him in an unsubtle fashion he will be able to deduce what you are doing, or are about to do. You must handle the opponent in a subtle and sophisticated fashion that does not signal your intentions, by not using strength and power too early and before you have really

caught him. For example, if you are using Nagare or are flowing from technique to technique, if you use too much tension or power here, you will signal to the opponent where you are flowing to. You will effectively remove the element of surprise. You can of course handle him in a way that makes him think you are clumsy and unsophisticated and are leading him in one direction, when in fact you are trapping him in a totally different direction.

I haved talked a lot about having the balance of mind to choose the correct technique for a given situation. However, at higher levels, so as not to be predictable or obvious it is better to select a not so appropriate technique deliberately, so as to deceive the opponent. You can now probably begin to see that in Ninjutsu nothing is fixed.

Kakehiki (Strategy)

Despite what a lot of people think, it is not wrong to achieve what you want, as long as you don't do any harm to anyone or anything – consider it as focusing on going from A to B in the most expedient fashion. Sometimes there are obstacles, such as obstructive people who are training partners or workmates – and of course there is your own ego. I always ask myself why these people are being difficult, and normally the answer reveals that there is a flaw or weakness in their psyche. I then think of how to work round this situation.

At this point it is helpful to identify what you personally want to achieve, and on occasions this would be easier with the help of these difficult people – so why not get them on your side? Often the reason they are being unhelpful is either jealousy or because they fear that you will become better than them – so for one reason or another, they feel threatened. If you show these people that you have a soft spot or even a weakness, you can usually get them to help you. However, the problem with this plan is that most people's natural reaction is not to please others by demonstrating any sort of weakness.

So how can we give everyone what they want? If you become more aloof and distant you will perpetuate the scenario. Being aggressive and 'teaching them a lesson' doesn't help solve things either, since by doing so, it positions you in a place of perfection, which is mainly hypocritical. So one proposal is this: that you mention to the person in question that you realize you have had your differences, but you acknowledge that they have skills you admire and would be very grateful if they could help you gain these skills for yourself. This will quell their fears of you being better than them, and will alleviate the threat, even if it is not true and you only do it to satisfy their ego. It also gets them to help and improve you, which is exactly what you want. Everyone wins.

With regard to fighting, it is always a good idea not to fight an opponent on their terms. For example, if they want to punch and kick, grapple with them, and vice versa. You should presume that the opponent is an expert of their favoured form of fighting, so don't confront them on their terms. It is very easy to determine which way your opponent prefers to fight, and that is by making an aggressive movement towards them and seeing whether they want to grab you or hit you. You should then do the opposite to them.

Perserverence

Perserverence is the quality of never giving up. As already mentioned, Hatsumi Sensei often says 'keep going', and he has also said that there is only one secret in Ninjutsu, and that is to keep training, and everything else will be revealed.

I have seen a lot of students with an abundance of natural talent, training alongside students with average ability. For years the gifted student has it easy and can do everything easily, while the other student has to continually struggle. However, as these two students become more advanced, everything by nature becomes more difficult – and at this point the student who is gifted often quits, not being used to dealing with incremental improvement and a struggle. But the less gifted student, who is accustomed to this continual struggle, just carries on as always and in the end far surpasses the most gifted students.

Within this situation is the issue for the student not to overtrain. Some new students want to train five or six times a week, but after a year or two they become disillusioned with the art and stop training, mainly due to the frustration of not being able to maintain the steep learning curve they had maintained as a beginner. Training should be considered like running a marathon, and you should pace yourself carefully.

Ki-Ai (Internal Energy Shout)

I have mentioned this topic earlier. There are two types of ki-ai: silent ki-ai and audible ki-ai. The silent ki-ai has already been mentioned in the intention section. The purpose of ki-ai is to cause doubt and discourage the opponent. The timing for a ki-ai is when the opponent is about to do a technique, and if you can get this timing correct you can completely unbalance him. It is also possible to augment your techniques with a ki-ai. This, in its basic form, is like a weightlifter breathing out as he lifts.

Mysticism

The esoteric skills are for some reason a subject that a lot of people want to master without putting in the requisite amount of training. But this is like a child having a loaded gun, with no ability to control his new-found power: he is a danger not only to himself but also to the people around him. It would be inappropriate to delve into this subject too deeply in this book, but be aware that there are chants using various tones, along with particular finger entwining, that can invoke mystical powers. Some people have delved into this on their own, and have ended up being quite disturbed. My own view on this subject is not to dabble with these techniques until you are very skilled in the physical aspect of Ninjutsu, otherwise you will open a door without any means of controlling what passes through.

Aruki (Walking)

Walking skills are vital in Ninjutsu as you need to move and also change direction quickly; the best way you can do this is to take quick, short steps. You should practise walking and changing direction in this way. Within Ninjutsu it is also important to walk

1. I keep my foot pointed as I place my toes towards the ground to feel for any obstacles.

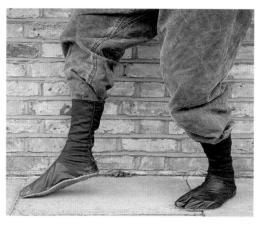

2. I have placed my toes down and am slowly applying weight, making sure this does not make any noise.

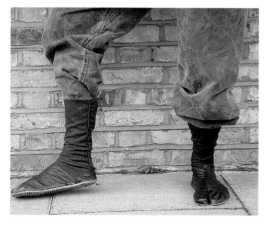

3. I have placed the weight on my toes and am now transferring the weight slowly down the side of my foot.

4. I have placed my weight on my front foot, and am preparing to lift my back foot. Note how my feet are no more than shoulder-width apart.

silently on noisy surfaces such as gravel and squeaky floorboards, or in darkness. This is best done by lowering your centre of gravity and taking very slow, short steps by placing your toes down first, and feeling the space where the foot is going to be placed for any obstacles. Then apply more weight progressively, making sure no noise is made and allowing the weight to transfer along the outside of the foot to the heel.

It is important to do this progressively so that if you make a noise you can stop and replace your foot and start the process again and find a spot that doesn't make any noise or doesn't have any obstacles. If you are walking across gravel, you should apply the same technique, but place the heel down first, and transfer the weight to your toes. As you apply your weight, you should keep tension in your foot so it arches inwards. The secret is to move slowly and disturb the stones as little as possible.

The other walking skill you need is to be able to walk on slippery surfaces. This is done by again lowering your centre of gravity and taking relatively short steps, and walking on the flat of your feet. You must avoid placing your heel down first as this can lead to a slip.

Another walking method is Yoko Aruki, a sideways walking method where you move sideways by crossing your arms and legs. If you want to practise this technique, start in Hira Ichimonji. To move to the left, cross your right leg in front of your left, while crossing your right arm in front of your left, in an 'X' position. Then step to the left with your left leg back into Hira Ichimonji, and repeat the process again. All the time your body should face forward; however, you should look to the back, side and front to make sure you can see anything unusual. This type of walking is very useful for covering a distance quickly while, for example, keeping your back against a wall. This would

be useful if it were dark and you needed to stay in the shadows.

Ma-ai (Distancing)

This concept has been touched on earlier, but is a really important issue while training. The student needs to develop a sense of distance rather than a calculated method of gauging distance. You should be able to look at an opponent and intrinsically know the correct distancing, and this should be the perfect distance regardless of the opponent's physiology or skill level.

As mentioned earlier, you should also be sensitive to the distancing between two people in a general way – that is, in a business or personal relationship, or in any other relationship. So you should consider person to person distance, person to objects, and distancing that exists through conversation. Distancing is really important in any give-and-take situation all the way through your life. If you make a mistake with Ma-ai it is possible to lose a conflict that should have been easy to win.

Ego, as we have touched on before, can manifest itself as poor judgement. When your ego desires something it can really disrupt your judgement when you are trying to maintain the correct distance. For this reason it is desirable to empty the mind Mu, or go to zero to give you the correct perception of a situation. Only through this type of practice will you be able to discern if people have hidden agendas, or, in a martial situation, if they have a hidden weapon or some secret technical trap for you.

Clearly there is also a different Ma-ai if you want to punch, if you want to throw, or have a specific weapon. This distance is also different if you are defending these particular situations. You should be able to judge this good distancing intrinsically. You should also be able to judge the distance between you and

1. Here I have my back to the wall in Hira Ichimonji No Kamae, and I am looking forwards.

2. I am moving to my right, but looking and checking to my left. Note how I am in a low position with my back square with the wall.

3. I am still moving to my right, and have gone back into Hira Ichimonji No Kamae and am looking ahead.

4. Still with my back to the wall and moving to my right, I am now looking and checking to my right.

101

the opponent and other objects such as stairs or steps, or things that can be used to unbalance the opponent, or impact the opponent into. The only way to have this all encompassing judgement of distancing is training, and there is no short cut.

Women's Training

Ninjutsu is highly suitable for women to learn as it does not rely on size and strength; it is easy for the smaller trained practitioner to prevail over the larger untrained person. It has been said that the ratio of strength of men and women is 7:3, so it is vital for the female practitioner to realize how important it is to use the man's strength against himself. This technique is called *Gosha Dori*, or catching a strong man, and means to use someone's power against themselves. The concept is to attack the parts of the opponent's body that are difficult to defend or strengthen, such as *kyusho* or pressure points. By continuously hitting these points, eventually it will take away the opponent's eagerness or spirit to engage in combat: this concept is called *Ateki*. Also being aware of the terrain and environment will be a big advantage in these situations. Knowing these things will hopefully give the person being attacked a chance to escape.

With regard to molesters, the Grand Master has said that the woman being attacked should see the molester as wild and crazy, and not consider them as human beings; treating these people as human beings may lead to a big mistake being made. This really means not to underestimate what this type of person is capable of. I mentioned earlier about people who cannot control themselves being no more than wild animals.

The female practitioner should consider striking sensitive targets such as the eyes, ears and face of the opponent within any technique, also attacking the small bones in the body, such as the bones in the fingers and feet, as well as the shins and groin, which are all delicate areas and painful when struck. Because of the disparity in strength it would be very unwise to compete on a strength basis and meet force with force, and anyway this would not be good Ninjutsu.

Kyusho Jutsu (Weak Points Method)

This is the method of manipulating the weak or lethal points (Dim Mak in Chinese) of the human body. Exactly where these points are varies from Ryuha to Ryuha, or school to school, although there isn't a huge difference. However, what is the same between the schools is that these points are painful when manipulated, and can have serious medical implications if struck with force or are hit in sequence. This latter information is beyond the parameters of this book, but suffice to say when you look at the sequence of blocks and strikes found in the San Shin No Kata and the Kihon Happo, in conjunction with the acupuncture meridians of the body and the implications, it makes very interesting reading.

A point that should be noted is that the effectiveness of Kyusho Jutsu varies from person to person. I have noticed that people who are double-jointed or over-flexible are often impervious to the manipulation of their *kyusho* points. Equally, *kyusho* points are often positioned differently from person to person, and familiarity and practice will help the practitioner find these points in different people. Again, if you are trying to attack a *kyusho* on an opponent and it is not working, you need to be able to flow into another technique.

There are *kyusho* that cause pain, lethal pain, that cause illness some time after being struck, and that cause a temporary reduction in your life force or Ki. Also there are other weak points that can make you immobile for a few days, immobile for a moment and those that just ache. With the help of the diagrams on pages 104 and 105 I will list the points and where they can be found. Please note that although the *kyusho* points on the chart are marked on one side, they actually apply to both sides of the body unless positioned along the centre line of the body. Please be aware that the knowledge of *kyusho* is useless without the Fai-jutsu to strike them correctly.

Kyusho Points

Tento (Heaven Head) This is the point at the top of the head. It is the area that is soft when children are born.

Kasumi (Fog) These are the temples on either side of the head. Due to the arteries and their proximity to the surface of the skin, this is a very dangerous area to strike.

Happa (Eight Leaves) This is the ear canal and also the ear drum. It can also incorporate the bone just behind the ear that protects the inner ear. Shock to the latter point can affect the recipient's balance.

Asagasumi (Morning Mist) This point is found under the bottom of the chin.

Gokoku This point is found in the middle of the back of the hand between the middle finger and the forefinger. It is the point used when performing Omote Gyaku.

Ryufu (Dragon's Wind) This point is found on the Adam's apple. Hitting here can cause swelling that could block the airway.

Daimon (Big Gate) This is the middle of the shoulder joint or head of the humerus, and if struck correctly can dislocate the shoulder.

Dokkotsu (Single Bone) These points are found on either side of the Adam's apple. If you hit the opponent's right side, it is more effective than hitting the left.

Jujiro (Intersection) These points are the front of the shoulder just below the anterior deltoid muscle, and on top of the clavicular part of the pectoral muscle.

Hoshi (Star) This point is found on the underside of the elbow. Striking here will have an effect on the opponent's grip and is very painful as it pinches the medial and ulnar nerve against the bone.

Jakkin (Weak Muscle) This point is found on the inside of the upper arm and is situated between the bicep and tricep muscles. It is possible to damage the median and ulnar nerves when striking here, and also therefore to affect the opponent's grip by hitting this point.

Kimon (Demon Gate) aka Omote Kimon This point can be found above the nipple and is the spot between the two chest muscles, the pectoral major and minor. This point should be hit in towards the spine.

Seitaku (Star Mud) This is the top side of the elbow joint, with the thumb up. Grabbing here can make the knees buckle and the head peck forwards.

Kage This is the protruberance at the bottom of the sternum called the xiphoid process.

Butsumetsu (Buddha's Passing) This is both sides of the ribs and is midway down the ribcage below the armpit. It is an area that is impossible to protect with muscle and also includes the end of the floating rib. The point should be struck in towards the centre of the body.

Gorin (Five Rings) These are five points situated around the belly button.

Sai (Crush) This point is on the inside and outside of the mid thigh. It has been said if you are hit here hard you can't stand up for a few days.

Kosei (Force of A Tiger) This point is the groin, specifically the testicles, although this area is a sensitive place for women as well.

Kyokei (Strong Tendons) These points are found on the top of the foot, just above the base of the toes.

Yaku (Press) These points are found in the middle of the calf muscle. It is extremely uncomfortable if you are hit here.

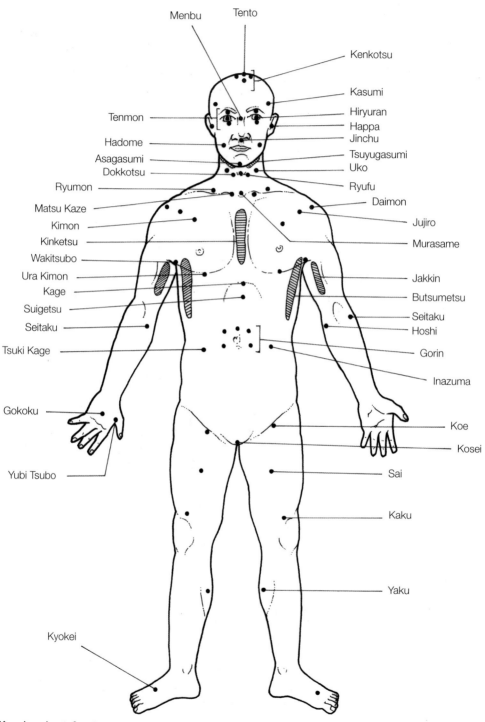

Menbu
Tento
Kenkotsu
Kasumi
Tenmon
Hiryuran
Happa
Jinchu
Hadome
Tsuyugasumi
Asagasumi
Uko
Dokkotsu
Ryumon
Ryufu
Matsu Kaze
Daimon
Kimon
Jujiro
Kinketsu
Murasame
Wakitsubo
Ura Kimon
Jakkin
Kage
Butsumetsu
Suigetsu
Seitaku
Seitaku
Hoshi
Tsuki Kage
Gorin
Inazuma
Gokoku
Koe
Kosei
Yubi Tsubo
Sai
Kaku
Yaku
Kyokei

Kyusho chart, front.

104

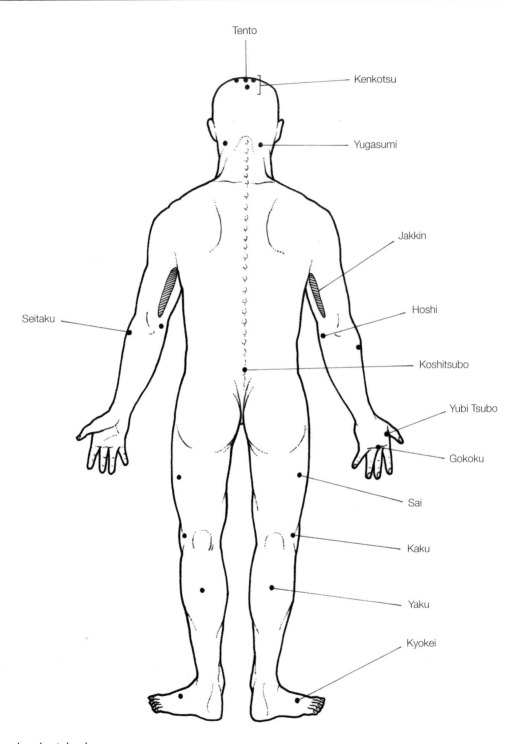

Tento

Kenkotsu

Yugasumi

Jakkin

Hoshi

Seitaku

Koshitsubo

Yubi Tsubo

Gokoku

Sai

Kaku

Yaku

Kyokei

Kyusho chart, back.

Kaku This point is the knee and the painful points on the inside and outside of the knee joint.

Koshitsubo (Hip Pot) You can find this point at the base of the spine where it joins the hip, also called the sacrum.

Koe (Voice) This point is between the centre of the thigh and the groin and is where the femur joins the hip. This point is also where the femoral artery and femoral nerve begin, before they run down the leg. It is possible to dislocate the hip if this point is kicked hard.

Yubi Tsubo (Finger Healing Point) This point is found at the base of the thumb, between the thumb and forefinger. It should be hit or squeezed in towards the forefinger.

Ura Kimon (Outside Devil's Gate) You can find this point on the ribs just below the nipple and below the pectoral muscles.

Suigetsu (Water Moon) This point is just below the xiphoid process and is the solar plexus. This area affects the diaphragm when hit.

Kinketsu (Forbidden Hole) This the length of the sternum and, again, is impossible to protect with muscle. This point lies over the heart and is very influential over the governing of Ki.

Wakitsubo (Side Bowl) This point is the hollow of the armpit where there are some lymphatic glands.

Murasame (Village Rain) This point is found in the notch at the top of the sternum. This point can be hooked or struck with the forefingers.

Matsu Kaze (Wind in the Pine Trees) These points are the inside ends of the clavicles.

Ryumon (Dragon's Gate) This point is the space behind the clavicle or collar bone, going down into the body.

Uko (Door of Rain) This is the side of the neck and is also known as Amado, and is a point found level with the Adam's apple just forward of the ear. It is close to the carotid artery, jugular vein and the vagal nerve that regulates the heart. It should be struck in towards the spine.

Jinchu (Centre of a Human) This point is the base of the nose and the top lip, between the nostrils. This point can be struck, but it is more painful if rubbed in a lateral motion.

Hadome (End of the Teeth) You can find this point by moving to the area where the back teeth or molars are; the muscle of the jaw is positioned there. This area also goes into the cheek tissue below the eyes.

Tenmon (Heaven's Gate) This point is the ridge of bone above and below the eye socket. It is sometimes massaged to alleviate headaches, but if pressed hard is painful and is useful in controlling the opponent's head.

Hiryuran (Flying Dragon Confuser) These are the eyeballs.

Menbu (Face) This point is the bridge of the nose. When hit it causes a reflex that causes the eyes to water, which affects your sight, *Metsubushi*. It can also refer to the face in general.

Yugasumi (Evening Mist) This is the sensitive point about an inch behind the lower ear in the base of the skull.

Kenkotsu (Healthy Bone) These are four points on the skull, positioned front, back, left and right of Tento on the top of the skull.

Tsuyugasumi (Drop of Mist) This is a point under the jaw line and is where lymphatic glands are situated. Also, just below the ear into the jaw is a very sensitive area.

Inazuma This point is found to the opponent's left side of their belly button.

Tsuki Kage This point is found to the opponent's right side of their belly button.

This subject has been very difficult to compile, as some of the *kyusho* points have historically been wrongly translated and named and positioned incorrectly on diagrams; also different schools either have different names for the same place, or they have the same name but found in different positions. The other issue is that some of the *kyusho* information available actually relates to non- Bujinkan styles, be it acupuncture points or completely unrelated martial arts schools. All these issues have made researching this subject extremely difficult. If I have got any of these points wrong I apologize, however, I have tried to be as thorough as possible.

Rules of Ninjutsu

The main teachings of Ninjutsu are:

1. Avoid violence
2. Ninpo is Bujutsu
3. Swear to be peaceful and protect your country, family, friends and nature

As we all know, violence is the cause of just about all the world's unrest, be it driven by religion, or by the desire for another country's natural resources. This topic will not be explored further as the author does not want to enter into a political discussion; however, on an individual level, the use of violence shows an inability to communicate in an adequate fashion.

We should consider the fact that these teachings are a thousand years old – and that even then there was a huge respect for nature and an understanding of the importance of being at one with it, that we in the West are only just beginning to comprehend. If everyone lived his or her life with these values, the world would not be such a bad place. The essence of harmony with nature occurs throughout this book, as it is a fundamental Ninja edict.

It is odd that the human race values the protectors of the weak, and despises those that take advantage of them. However, with our collective depletion of the world's natural resources, and our own failure to dispose of our waste efficiently, we are going to leave a hideous legacy for our children in the future – and this will be the ultimate exploitation of the weak. We should, as human beings, consider the planet as being on loan to us, and should leave it in the condition we found it, rather than pillaging its resources. A lot of the animals and landscapes that we enjoy now, will be lost for ever, and possibly even our children will not have the chance to see these wonders. As this art is so closely linked with nature, practitioners should make considered efforts to support the environment, and to use their influence, where they can, to this end.

In Conclusion

Lastly, I hope you have enjoyed this book. I apologize for having finished on a lecture. I have tried to make the detail as comprehensive as possible, and hope that beginners will use it as a reference book, and that higher grades will be inspired by some of the concepts presented. The practitioner should seek out a good instructor, as it is impossible to learn this complex martial art from a book alone. Each country has a list of instructors who can be found on the internet. If you are in the UK, my website is www.yeodojo.net

I would encourage everyone to try and get to Japan and train with the living source, Hatsumi Soke. It is a unique experience that you will remember for the rest of your life.

The martial arts give the practitioner the opportunity to be confident and live without fear, but to do this requires doing the correct preparation and hard work in the dojo. The talk and being artificially psyched up soon disappears once the pain of conflict begins.

Glossary

Aruki Walking
Ashi Leg
Atemi Striking

Bansenshukai A historical Ninja book
Bo A wood staff
Boken A wooden sword
Boshi ken Shito Ken, tip of thumb strike
Bu Warrior
Budo Martial way
Budoka Martial artist
Bujinkan Dojo Soke Hatsumi's style, comprising the nine schools of which he is the Soke. Divine Warrior Training Hall
Bujutsu Warrior Arts

Chi Earth, Chinese for Ki, internal energy
Chi No Kata Earth form
Chi Ryaku No maki The principles of earth
Chudan Mid level of the body

Daijodan A sword posture with the sword held over your head
Daikomyosai A training event celebrating Soke Hatsumi's birthday
Dakentaijutsu Methods of striking the body
Dan Black belt grades
Densho Book of techniques and principles
Do Way, path

Empi Elbow

Fu Wind
Fudo Immobility
Fudo Ken Immovable fist
Fudoshin Immovable spirit

Gambatte Keep going
Gedan Lower level of the body
Gi Japanese martial arts uniform
Gikan Ryu One of the nine schools of which Masaaki Hatsumi is Grand Master
Godai The big five elements
Gogyo Five transformations
Gyaku A reverse or twist
Gyokko Ryu One of the nine schools of which Masaaki Hatsumi is Grand Master
Gyokushin Ryu One of the nine schools of which Masaaki Hatsumi is Grand Master

Hakama Traditional Japanese pleated overtrousers
Hara An individual's body centre, just below the belly button
Henka A variation of a technique
Hicho Flying bird
Hidari Left
Hombu Dojo The head training hall, run by Soke Hatsumi; currently based in Noda Shi, Japan

Ichi One
Inton Concealment and camouflage
Irimi Entering

Jakkin A *kyusho* point on the inside of the arm between the bicep and tricep
Jodan Upper level of the body
Ju Ten
Ju-jutsu/Jiu-jitsu Gentle or flexible martial art; the forerunner of judo
Judo Gentle or flexible way, a grappling style created by Jigaro Kano
Junan taiso Stretching and body conditioning
Jutai-jutsu Grappling techniques
Jutsu/Jitsu Techniques, method or art. The latter suggests a more modern version

Ka Fire
Kaiten Rolling
Kamae Posture/form
Kazushi Balance breaking
Ki Internal energy; 'Chi' in Chinese
Kihon Happo Eight basic techniques
Kime Intention
Kimono Traditional Japanese gown; sometimes used to describe a *Gi*
Koppo Jutsu Methods to strike and break the bones
Kosshi Jutsu The art of striking organs and soft tissue
Koto Ryu One of the nine schools of which Masaaki Hatsumi is Grand Master
Ku Void
Kuji in Nine syllable seals
Kukan Three-dimensional space, and the techniques that can happen within this space. This can be between the opponents, but also in relation to objects surrounding Uke and Tori
Kukishinden Ryu One of the nine schools of which Masaaki Hatsumi is Grand Master

Kumiuchi A judo grip

Kumogakure Ryu One of the nine schools of which Masaaki Hatsumi is Grand Master

Kung Fu Chinese fighting systems

Kyo Jitsu Tenkan Deception, weaving of truth and falsehood

Kyokushin karate Mas Oyama's style of knock-down karate

Kyu Grade below black belt

Kyusho Vital or nerve point

Ma-ai Distancing

Metsubishi Sight remover

Migi Right

Mu Shin No mind, empty/clear mind

Mu To Without sword

Mu To Dori Unarmed against a sword

Nagare Flow/roll

Nage To throw

Ninja A practitioner of the art of Ninjutsu

Omote Outside

Oni Devil or demon

Ryu School, style or tradition

Samurai The governing warrior class in feudal Japan

San Three

San Shin A state of heightened awareness

Seiza Seated posture

Sensei Teacher or instructor

Shihan Master teacher

Shikan Ken A fist formed by folding the fingers at the second knuckles

Shinai A bamboo sword primarily used in Kendo

Shinden Fudo Ryu One of the nine schools of which Masaaki Hatsumi is Grand Master

Shin Gi Tai The balance of mind, body and technique/spirit

Shuriken Throwing blades and stars

Shuto Kiten ken, edge of hand strike

Soke Head of the house, Grand Master

Soshin No Kamae Similar to Ichimonji No Kamae, but the back hand is held at the hip in Boshi Ken

Sui Water

Sutemi waza Sacrifice technique

Tabi Split toe shoes used in training

Tae Kwon Do Korean kick-boxing

Tai Jutsu Body skills or techniques

Tai Kai Big meeting, the name for Soke Hatsumi's training meetings around the world

Tai Sabaki Natural body movement to evade attacks

Takagi Yoshin Ryu One of the nine schools of which Masaaki Hatsumi is Grand Master

Tobi Jumping and leaping skills

Togakure Ryu One of the Ninjutsu schools of which Masaaki Hatsumi is Grand Master

Tori To catch; the one applying the technique

Tsuki Punch

Uke A block, or the person who receives a technique

Ukemi Break falls

Uko A *kyusho* on the side of the neck

Ura Inside or hidden side

Ushiro Backward

Waza Technique

Yoko Sideways

Zenpo Forward

Useful Websites

www.bujinkan.com The Bujinkan Headquarters, Japan

www.bujinkanbritain.org Bujinkan UK website

www.bujinkankingdojo.org Peter King's website

www.yeodojo.net My website

www.winjutsu.com Bujinkan US website

www.hanako.co.uk Paul Richardson's website

www.bujinkanlondon.org Bujinkan Hammersmith Dojo website

Index

110